Neither Weak

Nor Obtuse

A Memoir

Jake Goldsmith

For Mum, Dad, and Ellen

"We are all so afraid, we are all so alone, we all so need from the outside the assurance of our own worthiness to exist." – Ford Maddox Ford, *The Good Soldier* (1915).

"We live in a world of abstractions, of bureaus and machines, of absolute ideas and of crude messianism. We suffocate among people who think they are absolutely right, whether in their machines or in their ideas.

And for all who can live only in an atmosphere of human dialogue and sociability, this silence is the end of the world." - Albert Camus, 'The Century of Fear' (*Combat*, November 21, 1946).

CONTENTS:

FOREWORD - TREADING WATER

AUTHOR'S INTRODUCTION

*

THE STRUGGLE FOR HOME

*

IN ABUNDANCE: REDUX

*

THE FAILURES OF DISCOURSE

*

PEOPLE OF RESPONSIBILITY

*

WHY I WRITE, WHAT I WOULD WRITE

*

CORRESPONDENCE, LOVE

*

THE END OF CHRONICITY

*

5

There is much that is said and written in the name of philosophy which operates at a remove from life. I refer to that variety of thought which seeks to divorce itself from the practical questions of life, and how to live. Jake Goldsmith's most recent work, which you are about to read, is exempt from this charge, as it deals with matters of life and living. It speaks of a quiet persistence and passing, of the acceptance and rejection of infirmity. His work is permeated by an opalescent refusal to give up, and instead commits to a search for truth and meaning, in a world which seems to provide none.

Some call this the art of living – it seems to me as good a term as any. It is this that I so admire about

Jake's writing. It is haunted by a difficult question which demands an answer. Once I was driving Jake back to his home and asked him a question I realised I'd never thought to ask him: "Do you think your interest in philosophy has anything to do with your illness?" He replied "Of course, because without it I drown." He didn't need to explain what this meant: I knew him well enough by then to understand.

Since birth, Jake has been ill: constantly medicated and plagued by routine clinical suffering, but most importantly, he has always been faced with the near-certainty of an abbreviated lifespan. Jake has Cystic Fibrosis, often abbreviated to CF. CF is a chronic, life limiting condition which results from specific genetic faults in two genes which code for the CFTR[i] protein. The CFTR protein is involved in maintaining and controlling mucus membranes in many of the body's systems, particularly the lungs and digestive system. In a normal person, CFTR controls these membranes, but in a CF patient, the membranes become thicker than normal, and the patient will usually have severe respiratory difficulties, as well as increased vulnerability to lung infections. The life expectancy for a CF patient is around forty-two in countries with strong healthcare infrastructures, but many die long before this. There is no cure, and the new generation of drug treatments like Lumacaftor and Ivacaftor are supposedly ineffective against Jake's CF, because of the rarity of his mutation.[ii] In Jake's case, his illness has decreased his lung function to between twenty and thirty percent, which makes many things I take for granted in my own life impossible.

Most people adopt an attitude towards their impending death that is essentially evasion or disbelief. For the purposes of someone who has not had the misfortune of having to live with a chronic illness like Jake's, death is merely a concept you observe in the world which crucially, only ever seems to happen to other people. To some, the inherent truth and necessity for death is a thought that either does not penetrate, or is not allowed to. It's much easier, after all, to merely live with the delusion that it won't happen to you – somehow. I firmly believe that this delusion is one that most people maintain as a way of coping, though they may deny its existence if asked. Jake's experience of living is constantly in resistance to death – to tread the water that threatens, with its infinite depths, an eternal drowning.

Jake has never been afforded this luxury of ignorance, and as a result, he's had to grow up somewhat more quickly than most. Long before I set about the business of serious reading, Jake would spend most of his free time at school in the library.

From the many authors he would go on to read, one emerged early on, to which Jake would apprentice himself, in a way: Albert Camus. There is much I would like to say about Camus, and how his work influenced Jake, but the most important and foundational thing that Jake found in Camus was his mission. That is, a commitment to finding truth in the face of absurdity, without collapsing before the feet of nihilism. In the meantime, Jake has set about accomplishing a similar mission: to continue to live and to think – to push the rock up the hill, if only to watch it roll back down.

Therefore, what *Neither Weak Nor Obtuse* offers us is not merely critical, but essential: the unique perspective on a life lived in defiance of death.

William Fear

AUTHOR'S INTRODUCTION

I am very ill. If someone is reading this memoir before knowing me, then that would be the first and most obvious thing to know.

I have something of a haughty and self-important motivation for writing a memoir, being relatively young, as I have the persistent weight of illness stunting my time to speak. I need a model of myself - to have a promotion of my worth - and so here is no small attempt at a testament to my life and constitution. This work is a show of my growth, of what I love, and some diagnosis as to why I would love those particular things.

This model doesn't have a remedial end, even if that could be discerned, but at least has something by medical necessity of an intellectual and physical prognosis.

There's reason for cautious clarifications. I'm having to revisit things and grasp my life as I can, without pedanticism, and neither can I live comfortably in forgetting things and living easily - as much as that is attractive.

I revisit things to show some awareness of my past faults, for a lack of care or empathy which pervaded, somewhat, the troubles of my youth as it would with many.

I once witnessed a man who claimed to have read all of Jonathan Swift's satire, yet he was still an arrogant and brutish so-and-so who would belittle anyone who did not do well in secondary school or further education. Arrogance comes easily if one can set themselves apart from their peers just by knowledge accumulation, and I could at least see that somewhere with a younger me. Hubris and immaturity seem more apparent then, even if the lens that sees that is blurred. I want to have in mind as the rest is written a correction of attitude or tone if not of all my contents. To be read as humble and with a necessary deprecation is my pressing wish.

There are things that can be ordered, reasoned, or finely accounted, but there are those things which are incompatible. And that is what this is. In one's mind must be that a thinker without paradoxes is a lover without feelings. I will try as I can to show what I feel, with all those addled contradictions, for what is perhaps a final time.

I could think of following the path of abandonment found in Rimbaud[iii], which comes to me attractively on harder days, or I could have a different variety of steadfastness when it comes to what I will be describing. To befit my well-being in this shortened life of mine, I am far better disposed to engage in personal readings of philosophy and literature than to be caught in the meticulousness of study. I was disgusted, worn-out, made weary and drained by university life and formal education. I failed to see why I was putting so much time and energy into the studious road when I was such an unpleasant student: talking beyond what I needed to, not staying in-line with a syllabus and at least half-appearing as an arrogant young man who thought himself above his station.

Only the factual constraints of my health, lacking wealth, parental wishes[iv], and not being able to be some free-wheeling layabout so easily kept me from packing up my things and leaving more quickly. But eventually the relevant people knew of my dilemma and helped me to escape.

I can only express gratitude and love for all their understanding and affection.

I may not ever come to the stage when I know what I want to do with my future - if it exists. But I do want to write, and that is all, for myself and anyone who'll read. I have no need for a long and aggravating study of canon figures to then improve my perception or outlook on literature and life.

The point is that to live like that, with deadlines and a need to be tidy, did very little to suit my bodily circumstances, and it is no less trouble, if not a more pleasant and freer experience, to not need to conform to a system I struggle to appreciate. I had plans to move to Bergen (Norway) to study. But with my time as it is, it would surely be better to just visit the place casually. The troubles to either of these callings (a life of action or not) are different, and I feel I can more easily, and with a healthier heart, manage with idleness and the burden of my own bounded freedom to a better degree than being always busy: physical business being something I have never appreciated. For a person whose only real aim is to write - if not, to do nothing - college or university would become unhelpful beyond (what the Americans would refer to as) the sophomore year. By that time one would know that further wisdom, not the compilation of information, comes from the personal and indulgent reading of those like Goethe, or Montaigne, and not the dry dissection, or vivisection, of impersonal work in a lab-setting - and from getting out in the world and living. Most of the rest of scholarship in academic philosophy, history, or even literature, often amounts to something paltry. Not so much *dead*, but lifeless authors in unread journals. It has the misfortune (a great one considering how worthy the subject can be) of being for prim, pallid and uninspiring young men who will end up either teaching or devoting maybe 30 years of their sterile lives to investigating some miserably obscure facet of life, unless they take the initiative to do something more inspired and less set in drudgery. That said, I cannot besmirch the better name of teachers – or professors. There are those of a different variety and process who I owe the dearest of gratitude. But to teach in the scholastic setting is something I'm averse to. It is a devotion I cannot buy. The educational life is otherwise used as a stepping-stone, by vague parameters, by the proto-student to achieve some sort of work. Better to study, work, and drink than work full-time and drink, maybe (?). If work is possible. Sure, scholarship is necessary; but it is not for me. So I write, without care for scholarly enterprise, and I try to relax for the remaining years in my rarer setting of not needing or being able to do things. In the final analysis, I felt I had to leave formal study. My health had suffered and I could not have continued it. I had to leave, with only minor regret, but I can at least say I did enjoy some of the company alongside it. Of what my writing would be, then; at base is a struggling and difficult demonstration of the intricacies of my personal journey when faced with all those many interior and exterior problems. It is not how to overcome or outpace these things, but how I may contend with them under what is possible. The first few sections deal more with my views on philosophy, thinking, and discourse a little divorced from *the phenomenology of illness*, while they're nonetheless linked, and the latter sections deal more directly on living with illness. It is a portrait of my life, so if you want to skip the more academic considerations you may go to the penultimate section.

I was given a touching description by a distant American friend: "Dostoyevsky's Underground Man tempered by the measured humanity of Camus' Dr Bernard Rieux[v]." I hope I can maintain this measure until my last words, as it would be an appreciable legacy.

THE STRUGGLE FOR HOME

It will take a little while before I express clearly what a deadly, chronic illness means for my inner feeling and how I relate with that to those who are closest to me. Before that I wish instead to address what illness means for my thinking in more abstract terms – as it ties so inextricably to my political and philosophical discourse. These first few sections work through concerns about my identity when relating to things that are not exactly *ill* in a personal sense and at a glance could seem unrelated to medicine and illness. Yet all of my discourse is linked tightly to a series of scrambled conclusions resulting directly from being so ill. I will describe how I then relate to my immediate environment...

I never had real emotion for my home; what I would call really moving emotion. I did so for the contents of my house, my family, especially pets, books, and the immediate surroundings where I lived; so you could say I cared for my home in that sense. But not for a nation or even so much a culture. After a while that scornful contrarianism, whether it was my fault or not, whether it was justified or not, was not comforting nor productive. I certainly didn't appreciate the prevalent sense of class consciousness present in Britain, at all levels, its imperial history, or its economy, but the fact that there were lots of things to dislike shouldn't have meant I disliked everything. What I have always appreciated at least in where I am from, were idiosyncrasies, small details, something just slightly amusing, or a general but meagre thankfulness that I was at least not someplace utterly dire. The problem, in this awareness, came in elevating my own character with the help of the outside, which was something I found I needed. But ultimately I was only ever interested in land, nation, or British culture and its practices in an offhand way. I was especially fearful of those who loved culture too much. They showed their hand historically, and it wasn't the best of results. What I did have passion about was egoistic, or detached from anything I was ever able to hold in my hands. Nor was it about theory, or the abstract. It was what others held in their hands, oral histories, the sensual, but given a life and experience. When I came up to those fronts primarily, and personally, I was left a little empty. I wanted the tangibility that others described when they spoke of all these objects and practices they loved, yet I felt estranged from.

It were as if descriptions of character were *hyped*, and I had expectations unmet that I knew were not overblown. I disowned most optimism, so had I really fallen to raising my hopes too high?

How am I to maintain myself in any sort of contentedness if I could not do it alone, where so many theories or ideas about interior conduct fell short, yet I found most of my outside options unhelpful? Passion for stretches of road or the foggiest heathlands was only ever captured on sad nights, in gloom, where the lone flights of obscure birds would provide a temporary light that I would not otherwise have: I used to enjoy ornithology. I had more passion for dinosaurs than for most other things when I was little, but it was not a *practical* passion Am I misremembering my past? These aspects of life are described so glowingly, enviably, I could not aim to emulate without sounding artificial, or like a thief.

I remember a keen interest in the natural world as a buffer to urban encroachment, but I was never a boy scout or some *Swallows and Amazons* type. I was too weak, physically, and hadn't the fortitude for those pursuits. I simply took delight in nature in a sanitised reflection. I memorised the illustrations of wildlife encyclopaedias and extracts from magazines with a zeal and depth, but my interactions with this world palpably could never extend so far. I was limited by my illness, and trapped like a dog in a corner. I sauntered carefully in autumn meadows and wept under trees at the sight of death. From birth I was destined for a future spent in the specialist clinic, and by seven I was a regular inpatient as was expected of my disorder. And while I kept an earnest interest in nature throughout my adolescence (surely it is still in me somewhere?) I had to later become accustomed to feeling aloof from the naturalist's course. Or any work. Or likely any conventional route and normalcy that could attach me to this ecosystem. I shifted into the mental seat of the sterile urbanite while I still lived in the countryside. I watched the silhouettes of nightjars in the late evening – briefly stumped by their metallic whirring - and spotted spoonbills on marshes; but this was not, (save the most gorgeous of limited experiences), ever a romantic ideal of dancing with wolves, sitting by Walden Pond, or killing squirrels for sustenance. It was eerily distant. My experience of nature and the country, like a veneer I could only glance past, was deeply important to my growth and gratitude despite its aloofness from me.

And I drifted away from this. I want nature to return to me if I cannot return to it. My walks are further restrained to urban jaunts or loitering in local woodlands, if I walk at all, and while I want to recover something it is not of fleshy naturalism per se. Did I have that anyway? I'd not want to recover that due to a fear I earlier described, where people love something too much and one would feel a guilt by association in loving that thing too. I'd want to recover, rather, however poorly sketched, an importance of natural place and natural character - even a revelry - that does not resort to the power and talk invoked in elections. Not the force of character through threats. It is a different vigour that would be described and wanted as my ideal. Through all of this youthful curiosity, tinged with the scent of hospital linen, I felt pressured to write down notes and ideas and occasionally collate them. Unlike what is conventionally described as awaking a philosophical interest, I had no care for *wonder* for its own sake. I was instead pressured a little begrudgingly to convey things rather than go mad, and I picked up some liking for a part of it [philosophy, or the history of ideas] along the way. What I found however was what I wrote, in observations of abstract theory or the world, always became biographical and unlike the common demand to be impersonal.

I have a literature of despair that I need to move past but cannot forget. I do not want the pessimistic attitude of Schopenhauer but I cannot forget Schopenhauer, and he is useful anyway. I still see sadness and grief left to be responded to reflexively, and dealt with in the worst way among emotions. A sure point: memoirs of loss, oneself, and a grief observed are numerous, and so I risk repetition and boredom. Yet what else am I to do but this therapy that doesn't exceed what is possible? Despair needs to be the penultimate word, where the last word is impossible. My entire work amounts to being a diary of a disappointed man, and I recoil equally as I embrace the only perception I can know - hung-up with my health and hurt without a real course to mend things. I at least want to illustrate my wishes, however poorly.

*

Say I go to the coast. I walk alone or with a friend along a stretch of cold beach, frequent a café, or try ice-cream despite the crisp air. This is an ordinary thing but one I somehow struggle with. What am I to say of this? At once, there is an immense gratification at the simple, yet also a bitterness, and when I spoke of my strange quandary, the subtle differences of a chronic life, of how I was not nor could be satisfied with myself in a simple setting at the day's end... was it alien to those I said it to?

Or would they articulate similar worries if not so busy?

I can try being a flâneur to forget my troubles but it loses charm without company to share in or time to write on it while travelling.

My problem with revelling in the ordinary, no matter what motivation I had to like it more, was that I held so earnestly, against my desire and my deepest wishes, something cool and sterile and firm about the outside world, which too I knew was not objectively possible. I always thought this was an idea of verisimilitude – the banal truth of reality. An empty world that was correct.

I had when thinking of ordinary and seemingly simple things an arrogant stubbornness that was childish, or that of a curmudgeonly old man. I would see this discord at my remove from things and felt so much despair at what I could never rise above. I would still be troubling myself over what was impossible, in events or my personality, rather than seeing the impossible for what it was and trying at what was at least possible. Nor could I convince myself very easily that nicer things would otherwise be there. I was always *divorced* from basic events, but never married in the first place.

I was so heavy-hearted seeing the world. I despaired as if I were Heraclitus[vi] in this most trampled way, and one that felt pretentious and snobbish. I desperately want a love for my friends, as an expression to fend-off a world that could look like Zapffe's *The Last Messiah*...[vii] I could hear the cackling laugh of Silenus[viii]. It was there so clearly and I wept at it to the point that it hurt my bones. I didn't want that image of the world.

I had to find my summer.

*

I have a distinct young memory of a spindly tree - preserving its blossom before autumn in rural

Suffolk. It was quintessential, an easy subject for painting, and likewise easy to be pretentious about. I cannot place this with definite geography, but I remember absently staring at this picturesque tree caught in the biting wind. I was struck by the perseverance of the blossom in the wind. It seemed that every year it had to withstand the rain and wind of a dull Britain, like I did, and it fared better. I somehow linked this picture to something, imaginatively, like a child's fairy story or fable, as something I would recover only later to be literary and make a point about. I stretched it into a metaphor that I forgot and would not lead so consciously - about our use of and relation to the natural world. Most would not see this tree, but in distinguishable ways. Either *too much* was read into the beauty of the tree, its artful value, any spirit; false personifications, thus seeing past what was there in material truth - or it was ignored as a vaguely pointless thing, an ordinary and worthless fixture, not even worth study, where no pretentiousness should be afforded. Yet I want to afford it, I'm urged to, in my own endeavour, in reaction both to those that wouldn't see things and those that would see things too extremely; and so misreading the world. This reflects not just on our relation to, say, the natural world… but in how one relates to illness and sympathy. What we have is the tendency of some to attribute too much significance to things that otherwise really do have some amount of significance. When people read too much into things, there is a kind of loss due to an addition. On the other hand, people also tend to do the opposite and find no significance in things that merit very little attention, despite really meriting it. In a phenomenology of illness, this very basic point has a lot of power and I don't think it can be overstated. This is, to me, a root cause of the problems which face me. Relatives and friends may read too much into your pain. They might try to help you too much. You don't want to be suffocated with sympathy. At the same time, you deserve some level of sympathy and recognition for what is actually going on with you. It would be one thing if people could take one look at you and understand everything there is to know (i.e. all the relevant information and history which explains your current condition), but that is not the case. People don't know unless you bring it to their attention. This serves to perhaps generate even more confusion if you fail to convey things properly. So then there is the wish to not say anything at all, in order to save others from misunderstanding and thereby giving you either too much care or not enough. But if you stay completely silent, while perhaps preventing you from ever being wrong about anything, it is almost guaranteed that no one will notice the pain you endure, and your silence results in stagnation. This problem extrapolated into wider concerns certainly gives us some doubt and fear. The ignorance of this simple nature, an ignorance represented by neglecting something so ordinary, would not see a world delighting in being left to moral or ecological calamity; overlooking destruction; and the reactions of the distressed; too bothered by all that they could not solve, answer to impose their own poison.

I saw a double-threat from two false premises - even if it only manifested prominently in my vision rather than in physical practice - from both sides of an imposed divide: that of obfuscating spiritualism and sterile reason. Those that felt too intensely and those motivated coolly with disinterest. The romantic sensibility against the indifferent sensibility.

A gulf is enforced between them, and my mental effort would be to establish a truth between those commonalities. This schism isn't wholly Manichean, that dualistic view of good and evil, but the most

worrisome of ideas and people proposed that dark
and divided scene.

The threat is maybe, perhaps, only my own struggle
in how to see. But I could not maintain a sort of
solipsism and say other perceptions did not align with
that which I detested. Perhaps the most complete
apathy or indifference would be a more looming
threat, but the self-satisfied, with these paragons,
filled me with more fear. I later translated my
memory of blossoms into an attitude, held tautly,
there for rebuking many misgivings.

This was a dim oppression I saw. It wasn't a specific
violence or marked aggression against me - which
was foreign to me; it was a general despair concocted
heavily with my own frail body and disease. I could
not weigh sufferings against each other as quantities,
I could not score with these, but I had a prop that my
world would build around.

What are the enemies of this oppression? What Nietzsche referred to as *oppression*. I struggle to express them without sounding puerile. I had the ghastly reflection of the world's terror, and my sad observation, but there lurked beneath, as if I would class it as a nemesis... a breed of pride, a taste, force of character, that couldn't just lurk as some bad thing. Something that I would mistake for belonging to detestable causes by not finding my own definitions: by not declaring the fluidity of these words and eliminating their malformed associations or those who used them threateningly. There are virtues we need, disassociated from guises, which we can ineptly choose to best suit us. That make use of tastes that can be easily misused. The last century had this same problem, as did the one before, and my words could seem like some form of moral posturing. As well as being self-evident or common sense. If I were, I wouldn't be too fond of it. Posturing morally, especially, is a bit of a dirty thing that doesn't fix much. And as I hope to describe later it is distinct from good moralism.

My attempts to reawaken or rediscover *character* or *pride* are not hung-up on bringing back past affectations, nor found in kinds of traditionalism – the dead faith of the living that gives tradition a bad name. They would demand, personally, a removal of things when we harken to past deeds - a situating of persons and contexts. A type of history that wasn't supernatural while also not bereft of colour. There's too much in this world, I cannot account for it all here, and my personal survival requires ignoring things and specifying others. I do not want a force of brute, colloquial power; of campaigns expressed in mean slogans. But an almost natural vigour and love of nature we leave to be mistreated by kinds of political fetishists. It is the vigour that makes the blossom withstand rain that becomes the poetic aspiration.

The next set of troubles shows the arduous course of maintaining aspirations when faced with mean oppositions.

*

I am still in some part averse to feelings for my home, if not for the feelings of others for their own distant places. There's an envy there, as much as reproach for the most zealous.

Britain has a perfidious history, sometimes not seen within itself, yet one I would unfairly hold in my sight and not seem to shake-off from the possibility of my own mere self-love. Again, I was affected too much by the outside to be left alone in finding my own worthiness. Love for this place can manifest well… there is a certain beauty to the woods, the heaths, and the coasts I cannot deny, of their richness or minor glory; there's even that which passes for mountainous terrain. There's a wide selection of people who may as well be noted. But it is easier for this adoration of places to reveal itself in hubris, measuring injustice against injustice, where banal but severe temptations are lost in frustration and abandoned to excesses – the blight of violent adorations expressed without temperateness.

I want to show this place love: to refine me, my workings... I want the invincible warmness described as felt when basking in mild sunshine; the scents of unknown flora and the sounds of early winds, I want to sense these details of the world without the thought that I am succumbing to a clichéd experience - where I need enter another emotional universe to escape feeling embarrassed. I'd not want to be associated with such mockeries that misprint the world. I cannot live in a world unto myself. I need the outside to be comfortable too, and yet I cannot rely on it so greatly or otherwise delight in the upcoming calamity to feel good. I appear stuck. I should learn to be less put-off by the mismanaging of the world by and for others, especially if I half-assedly talk of some Samuel Beckett-tinged *quietism* on occasion.

What I want… In the morning, fresh moisture on the ruins; something young on what is ancient. Being somewhere, transient, with an old wisdom that doesn't harken perniciously. And then passes. It's the idea of a past that could be revelled in but not exaggerated, or tied to false foundations, with a simpler life in its present. There lies my imaginative attraction.

*

There's a point that will recur in a refutation of something. On finding one's own comfort we have outside alliances and attachments to the material. Land. Oceans. The Sun. People. And so we should care to better reflect what *material,* sensual attachments mean.

We begrudge the materialism defined by excessive greed for properties and luxury, and we should begrudge those narrow-chested lives, but that is not something we can take as a standing to denounce the idea that our baser belongings, and *materials*, are invested in our worth and memory. More so, people. When lacking belongings they may either become even more vital or one may attach less significance to what they would not be able to experience. You might envy nothing. To lose belongings, especially those hard to replace… it is obvious how this viscerally affects us and we should be more honest to not deny this. But we try pretending to be austere spiritualists when faced with loss and say one can do without things; that we may live just with immaterial

41

ideas and hopes, and then take that to another place
that is further unjust in allowing people to be without
mundane and worldly things. One would look to
another with nothing, as if that would give peace to
your having lost something. Only rare sorts can extol
in that type of solitude. It's evident that for myself, or
most, we seek attachments and investments in objects
- which are lesser forms of investments in people - to
help amount to our own being and attest to our own
being. And surely the world is too cruel for us to be
asked to live *so* modestly? We find little comfort in
an internal essence, soul, or whatever your position
would call it, on its own, *alone*, with no readings or
reciprocations and things it has lived up to and
within. With no shoulders to stand on. Or belongings
it has memory in. We are infected by secondary
knowledge while we are alone.

If I lost this entire writing in the process of
its creation I would be distraught and lost, and it

would be far too difficult to replace despite its comparative brevity. It would probably not be repeated, and I have a timeframe. The same distress one would have if they put time and bleeding effort into a film or project of work, a belonging, that was then lost. If such art, writing, and other creation was not you (your body and person), even, it was obviously part of you and your effort. It was a material testament of you, to you, or something which you looked to in order to prompt memory; something you simply used and spent time with that would be hard to replace. Yet we would speak as if things were easy to replace – as if we really did live in a world where such things didn't matter so much, despite our actions, our greed, and dominant cultural infrastructures.

Person or object – there is diversified pain to such loss; and it is cruel to deny the pain of those losses by measuring them up to others or by a rudimentary religiosity, denying the pain of things repulsively as we can outright do when drunk on ideas or in some bad mood.

Simply; place, items, commodities, are important as people are important, in their own degree, and we should deny less our frailty in our need for things. If I have an ontology and a metaphysics that is rather bare, too, I have recourse to sensual moments but with provisos and conditions. The *aesthetic life* is often not enough, but what of the others? Whether a materialist (I'm not too convinced I am regardless of the above) or a philosophical antithesis, there is the importance of place. The hollowing and critique of place, one's own place, spiritually or politically, needs to have prudence in its direction unless it wants empty results.

Objects, one's background, one's country, et al, are impressed upon to help us, and may be abused

as any idea or anything would be, and it is soon
unbeneficial to be critical yet not affirmative. We
succumb to puritanical denials of our need for
ordinary objects and peoples, and look for inadequate
replacements. To face a world of shattered atoms
alone? We can recognise gratuitous material greed,
obsessive nationalism, and naked hedonism for not
being too satisfying at the end, but that does not mean
we return to an opposite state of self-imposed vagrant
humility or another extreme in our critique of a
certain thing – lacking a temperateness or real
moderation.

It is obvious that most live in compromises
between them, but moralisers want to live extremely.
The result is a critical living but one without deserved
attachments. And what attachments are then
inevitably found, instead, are shallow or desperate –
and then dangerous in that desperation. Especially

when we speak of ideological and diplomatic attachments and assurances.

I need a type of materialism, and I cannot have some vague spiritualising that denigrates me and says I don't need things, must do it all myself, or can do without the outside with enough effort. Or that I must wholly rely on others for my care. That sort of aimless criticism doesn't help eventually. We live one way and speak in another to try and forestall our mistakes - failing to see that some of how we would live does not merit condemnation, if maybe sympathy, and we wander in our inward paradoxes. I will miss lost objects. I can maybe get over them or replace what is easy to replace. I will lose people and myself. That is a greater degree. If you lose a friend, you lose how your other friends would react and be with that person - a whole part of them now locked away. That intimate behavior fostered by another presence is now all gone. Why are we denying how

46

we are so affected by exterior things? We fail again and again at being insular people making ourselves only with ourselves. I find most supposed examples poor, and only a few persistent people really manage to be so austere yet remain true. What is secondary to us is there, outside, beating, making its own account, and unless we are so meek and confused how would we dismiss what contributes to us? In solitude. That exists. We also need solidarity.

I speak of *belongings* in my failure to find better words, and in doing so I am, admittedly, frustratingly vague in my definitions. I mean when I speak of belongings all those aspects of place included in a person's own identification, and the question of how much one is influenced by exterior events (nation, society, etc.) or by one's own solipsism (personal/intellectual growth and growth in spite of the former). That question, and its breadth, means all from books you own to how you feel about a town or city - how otherness that is physical contributes to you internally - that I will still not so simply call *immaterial* influences. I'm holding physicality to be the core and vital aspect, but I won't reduce it all – starkly - to a bland sort of *physicalism*.

I know I am trying to make a tenuous link between a nuanced idea of physical materialism, and then how to personally cope with people's perversions of abstract cultural ideas in ways that are extreme on either end. I have a strong feeling that that this whole presentation is philosophically primitive and I am unsure how to word it without a bland appeal to authority. Do I hold an untenable position, far too nebulous and unsure, and must we have instead a stable foundation established and untarnished by living contradictions? Sadly or not, I vacillate between my contradictions – in this specific attachment to my home, and more generally - and it is rather an ongoing conflict in philosophical position and personal worth, a passionate type of uncertainty, that gives the image of my world.

Why am I so bitter and conflicted in that I cannot enjoy, so easily, one's physical place? Why am I so uncomfortable? It is all I have – ourselves in physical place. Or all I can see. I've never had any time for a transcendent or heavenly world to escape in and so less is given to you, instead, in this cooler, indifferent reality which I have, a little begrudgingly. It is then harder going when, without that sort of spirit, we would gain equally harmful but linear religions and different ideological certainties trying to fill the empty gulf. This mundane world gains a vital aspect, if it is the only thing I can have, and how am I to find my worth in it without resorting to crude certainties, lies, or a more absolute sort of quietism or rejection? If your home has a history, even if you do not care for it, it means others will care and will impact you; act upon you. And we can't all live like hermits to escape that. I have to contend with this societal fact even if our world is meaningless, or perhaps, because it is, meanings will be perverted by my neighbours and I will need to deal with it. I can't escape into solitude to avoid misused meanings, I can't escape in faith or blissful ignorance, and so I'm having to burden myself with this conflict.

Culture will contribute to your survival and character even if you are hardened against words. And nor can I, again, so flippantly shake-off external influence.

There will be reservation and bemusement when your place and outside assurance, your home, is abusive or used to make trouble. This means the improbability there is in saying I could do so assuredly without where I happened to have been born and grown up. Even if I would sometimes want to be without it. This does not mean excess *pride* or feeling so proud, but feeling an acceptance of both our natural and national

50

agencies, at least the least unjust. I would have statelessness but it is unavailable to me, and it would be a posturing gesture were I to go for it. Denying and ruining your own history for so long from an intellectual's armchair starts to erode you, having a broad past affect a personality perniciously, and so those condemning their own place appeal politically to another that they don't know rather than knowing how to amend where they are now. That's the extreme but common reaction to not liking one's own seat.

My struggle to appreciate my home - both politically and philosophically - would not be about any grand diplomatic fix, nor historical pride (which has done enough damage), but being given the courtesy to feel quietly comfortable in the place I have to stay after I've bashed it for so long. If one wants to, then still keep note of what is pernicious. But in the desperation to fix where I live I should try not to stray into worse oppositions where I think an enemy of an enemy is somehow a friend. Not finding 'the grand fix' (or denying its existence) doesn't mean I shouldn't cultivate my own garden and a place where I can feel well - rather than reflecting dourly and ineffectually on all the very obvious flaws of Britain.

I will still betray my country before I betray my friend, and I don't *identify* with it in that common way. I just want a measure of what I can realistically do within it, *how* I might contend with living in it alongside its people, and of what isn't really very helpful in admonishing it. Because, realistically, I won't be going anywhere and I have some real limitations in what I can do.

Such fetishising of history, by friends and enemies alike, shouldn't stop personal reprieve - or the finding of a synthesis between excess patriotism and cultural admonishment. Between a fetish love and an obsessive hate. The problems of exaggerated national pride are obvious; those of national disgust contribute to wavering morale when it would be needed most in times of crisis, but also are exposed as voices: fine to slag-off their own place to the point of death and deny their lineage, while finding allies in those distant to them who'd soon throw them under the bus with no second thought, and who in their desperate allying, fail to see more terrible affairs. Sponsored tourists walking obliviously through Ukrainian famine…

The profusion of voices makes even liking this place, with its ideals, stale. Its niceties and finer beauties can be lost in files and bookkeeping, in futile arguments with strangers, and I am unsure, then, how to amend my hankering for caring about what is thought of as sensations. Am I unable to overcome the abuses of others when facing something that should deserve affection? They achieve that multifariously, these places; they achieve affection

easily by many who would not see to see; by many

who do not know how to love a place, nature, their

home turf, without rudely squandering it and so

corrupting the possibilities of national allegiance.

These places, too, face scorn which is unbecoming.

To hope for things becomes unwise, while to

languish in despair becomes foolish.

I want to return to my home and feel safe on its

beaches - unsullied by the misuse of pride.

IN ABUNDANCE: REDUX

The mass profusion of content and paraphernalia in the modern world works (as it can) against an idea of appreciation for one's residence. While recanting an old motif, this passage is also an expression of and reflection on modernity. In what that does for one's own worth if they are concerned for their own esteem, what trappings and bearings contribute to their self-esteem, and if they want to give a sense of real feeling in their oral history as opposed to a dry re-telling of history (a basic chronology), with little context or situation.

Given that this is supposed to be an indulgent memoir, I am concerned with how I feel

55

with and reflect on the situation I can distinguish –
and as the modern world is a slippery beast I'd want
to give (as I can, if clumsily) an impression of how
its contents affect me.

*

A new, exponential abundance of media and
infrastructure fashioned from the technics of present
civilisation means you are situated in a disordered
place, or at least one that has lost the illusion of
order.

Multifariousness means enough pros to
living in a new space, but equal cons (something
vapidly obvious), and a removal of an idea
sometimes seen as ineffectual, even churlish, but
something nonetheless important and taken to
extremes - which is *novelty*.

This is the essence or the quintessential idea of a place, commodities, people, or oneself, that is too easily perverted by nostalgists, the puritanical, or those who have a false, inept sense of history and what something was supposedly before. If we are to portray in a better light what this essence is, what appreciation for our places should be, then we need to remove from its equation those who misuse words for blunt propagandist motives.

These are fancier words for saying there's too much, and the case of more and more meaning less and less. It's not a height of pretension to say that many voices and their heightened noise can sully a place and hinder a personal connection. But we cannot go about rude and idealistic directions in trying to somehow amend these perceived dangers. It is a world of bombardment that would drive one to madness if not for sufficient psychological defences or evasion. Today things happen so fast that a mind

57

struggles to absorb them. Art begins to fail in conveying things. I have spoken of this before with exampled detail, yet wish for a dewy-eyed reiteration.

There is no heightening or relegation of quality ('*goodness*') in this new content, these cultures. This is not explicitly an ethical judgement of the past as somehow much better or much worse. To judge that is a deeper case than a resolute condemnation of all of one period. Too many people condemn the past or discredit the present with easy words, reducing the world to a single formula or a single conspiracy. What should be praised as well as smeared requires more than one explanation. It requires a depth that most would prefer to neglect for their ease.

Overall, in modern history, I will only say there exists the same sort, the same uncertain degree, of *quality* in the tabloid and the populous as well as in niche or contrary cultures: as in some vague idea of a relatively consistent beauty *and* a steady rate of filth. Gossip always was as bad. It is difficult to apply a coherent historical measure to the changes in media, and many would do so far too anachronistically. The artistic quality of cultural artefacts in different eras remains mostly consistent, though not by a formal measure; as to truly measure it would be entering a confused territory and banal subjectivity - a personal aestheticism. Was the media and catwalk fashion of the 1920s better than that of the 1980s? I will not say, just that I obviously have my own preferences. There were some obvious cultural and technical improvements that go without saying, but some things can be said to be worse for more insidious reasons.

When *1984* came about Huxley's *Brave New World*, published over half a century earlier, seemed more prescient than Orwell[ix]. What we loved would likely kill us over what we would rightly hate… So this isn't a question of a boorish politics or empty statistics. That can be seen as improved or diminished by one's biases. It is instead a nebulous question of artfulness and the amount of attention one can afford to art, and so it amounts to preferences for gossip focus.

The problem being diagnosed is what happens when you have too much of a *quantity of culture*, a different marketing of culture, and what population growth and overconsumption, and over-production, means for the exposure and portrayal of arts and individuals not just ethically, but by what attention you can afford to give them. What happens in the banal case when things are faster? What does quantitative growth mean for the attention to quality?

What does the modern world mean for culture when there's more who can contribute? It can mean that just as much, or more, by numerical quantity, fine and wonderful things exist; but by the nature of modern representations, mass media, etc, there is less of a weight and collective status so readily available to figures, celebrities, ideas, or places. And this can be seen by some reading as a loss of *novelty*. Or *Quintessence* [c.f Walter Benjamin][x].

Modern technologies mean the ability to proliferate far more of anything [media content] far more easily, which means the growth of further dishonest content (which is mostly always easier to create and propagate) alongside the steady growth of informational means. The lowest denominator in a culture will always be met and so we see a plague of base content as the means of art and creation are democratised and more easily available than before. This is a difficult explanation because one does not want the simplest denigration of a culture, the modern consumer landscape, and fine research and stories are still extant; they are just harder to find in the larger haystack of digitisation - with a broader, diffuse press, and with greater content creation. The creation of algorithmically tailored echo-chambers being, in cases, even more of a restriction on what one would see than a world only in *print* is another story... The fabrication of an ideological singularity.

The viewing figures of a television programme during the last century would often be higher than our new popular showings as there were, at a point, only 2-3 TV channels (UK), fewer radio stations, and a smaller press.

They would receive a higher consumption by default from the size of the population.

More choices mean different centres of attention and often a type of paralysis created by one's breadth of choices. There was a different type of celebrity-focus when the means of media production were lacking and differently regulated. More specifically, *public intellectuals*, people of letters, with a reach and influence (fame) could be said to have benefited from their technological regulation - as we now have the proliferation of online *pundits*.

Philosophy probably isn't dead and nor will it die (though for no lack of professionalisation's trying), ideas and movements won't die, but well-known and credible *philosophers* are perhaps the casualty of academic trends and the shifts of a wider televisual culture, with people now closeted from public appreciation. This [the priority of focus] is what could be missed by us, though we should bar any harking sentimentality. This case, this point in history, cannot be returned to – and nor should we try to - but there can be a reasonable wish for different attentions.

What was hitherto a majority consideration, a popular programme, may now be relegated to a niche interest in the popular world - though its numerical support is still at least present as it has an audience to sate it. Yet while it may be served, an idea, by equal numbers, it does not mean that - proportionally - shows or books or people are given the same fraction of coverage and publicity - and you may see in that a problem for the dissemination of ideas and, more vulnerably, cultural linkages and stability (both personal and public).

Old media meant products could be widely seen, but products were still confined in their number by technological ceilings, which thus determined and formed the boundaries of a culture. New media means there are more and more products, just as wide or wider, and far less restriction. This new era of anomie and wider *choice* will obviously have its harmful effects; though in noting that, and in the same breath, one should not revert to reactionary functionalisms or misplaced traditionalisms that proclaim the decadence of new culture and the need for dreamy returns – *ideological* or not. The case for the defence of modern *atemporality*, the defence of today, and the supposedly opposed case for rooted old ideas are often equally tragic and unoriginal.

The new millennium gave us not just new tools for a culture to use, but a new place for culture to live within and be used by. A change of priority in what is *celebrity* [i.e. what is often the focal point of how a culture appears], now long-evolved past our first Byronic conceptions of modern celebrity, and the continuing fashion of visuality as prominent and pre-eminent over text (no matter the profusion of new text and podcast) is seen as a symptom of technological-cum-cultural shift.

It seems boring and self-evident to say, but it does not discredit the possibility of new tools just because there are poor uses and troublesome focuses. Celebrity is something that can be enjoyed and used well. It is not a concept so wholly negative (it is simple to say we crave it as much as we reproach it), and we also take for granted how the people we popularly venerate are the measure of a culture.

Under a culture of technical limitations a product could be afforded more weight and influence as it was not stuck in a so huge a mass of different sources. There's a revolt that disposes of old orders, however terrible, that has many new outlets but with no suitable replacements for how to root ourselves (re: the civil unrest of May 1968), and has an ongoing process of finding out what the hell anything is or should be – that often fails. It would be easy to accept crude demagoguery or some other rashness to save you from uncertainty.

In shorter terms, there is no moral nostalgia that I have, as such, for a wet-dream of a past age where quality or morality was improved. That would be spurious and that is not what I have in mind. My nostalgia, my harking, shows itself rather as a mild, sometimes throwaway attraction to particular moments, the history of some memories or ideas, some people; and instead the feeling of distinct cultural perceptions, the need for roots but a prudent use, and descriptions we could still enjoy - not facile archetypes - while being displaced and moved in the mass of crowds. Instead of lost entirely.

There were always equal wonders and horrors, but our problem [mine] is we have an age of the newest filmic, reporting, sharing, and useful technics. I cannot abide a full Ludditism, technophobia, as some instinctual reaction to cruel societal changes. Fervent neo-luddites, neo-puritans, are not palatable. *The Anti-Sex League*, all the religious zealots of a secular world... they would all be mistaken in their diagnosis and cruel judgement of modernity. But there are other prospects that are likewise, if less bleak.

With our new *technics and civilisation*[xi], we have the muddling, disorientating cases where never before would any of these sorry sorts have been able to say anything offline, previously, beyond the effort to write letters of complaint. The consistent ignorance or unawareness of a public would have been, with whatever benefits and dangers that has, restrained. Almost nothing now exists without the invitation for public comment – without a near-instantaneous (and useless) public response. Now one can freely, with an effortless touch, with no mind or tact, violently say what one impotently thinks when nobody need speak. More than they ever would have done (as they surely would) before, not harming the community while sat at a bar, rather than online. And this bad talk is obviously not something I don't suffer from too. It doesn't help us so much. We're still as isolated no matter how well-connected. There's enough space for constructive work from actual constructive comment as well as what is utterly banal or rude, or even violent, if an author of an article or some such thing is tactful enough (shaped by an audience's response), but the existence of such near-omnipresent shit accompanying anything - which would be neither functional, critical, nor positive... but thoroughly pointless...

It may as well be said that I have a parochial reaction to it [the public] that could make me arrogant in my dismissal of such dismal people. And I sense I have to guard myself against those instincts. They've been given [the general population] the greatest ability in the history of publicity.

There should still not be so much of a barrier to the real questioning of things or growing to be a thoughtful person in discourse regardless of formal education, or lack thereof - though that is a rather common or obvious truth. Our openness is good there. You don't have to be in an ivory tower to be able to see and make change. Though people with qualifications still make ridiculous judgements (we can take John Adams'[xii] assurance that many great writers have said some nonsense) and now we have the added burden of people who have nothing good to say, or nothing to say at all, thinking they are deserving of a discourse rather than sound-boarding ideas and learning, and having some modesty, before they think they are deserved platforms or money for nothing. And the *undeserving* will get it. We at least used to have less of this thought of self-promotion because there were fewer means of attaining it. There were more confined editorial standards (for better or worse), and people would accept their imposed quietude - if querulously.

The messy point of this is trying to describe the problems of a modern culture without glorification nor with a cruder dissatisfaction when we are reflecting on the obtuseness of modernity and publicity. In our modern world we get the celebrities and the intellectuals we deserve, if we are being cynical.

Our so open and loud-mouthed people could at least make a minor effort in their thought and calculation rather than spend empty words in more of a picture exhibition than a substantive characterisation. Though that's perhaps a hope too far... Fetishism and mass media don't often allow a reflective intellectual pace - with the constant need for debate and spectacle. Could we even escape the society of the spectacle?

With the contemporary world mass saturation arrives. Slowing down to reflect goes awry when surrounded by zooming things. And I want something reflective over something so hurried. It is in some way a primitive wish. A quickened culture, as well as one of mass quantity, neither reflects nor understands itself very well. It fools itself into thinking it must move so very quickly, move away from history (good or bad, or act as its illusory culmination), that it will be safe as it is, or even believe that its racing will lead to success and a new world order; not realising the extent to which people hold ignoble grudges from their history - or crudely against the new world – nor seeing the strength of an enemy that might dislike their rushing. An *enemy* who themselves may be corrupt too in their reactionary tastes. People on any side of these perceived, multifarious divides don't take too much care.

Even if there were less understanding before, and one would now be more capable of information gathering, said information will not have the time or space to be ruminated on, and it is in constant danger of being overtaken again and again by something new. To be slow and pensive is not some unprogressive antonym to needed change or progress. It is a mistake of sensibility to think that opposing a hyperbolic rush would mean to oppose a necessary direction of moral or societal evolution. How is it controversial to wish to be more considerate and careful with how and where we step? The idea that a more contemplative speed could be contentious or even condemned as *conservative* - and against our interests - is the mistake of hurried implementations, some themselves reactionary or opposed to true reform, that have fallen prey to an anger that cannot cope with the world's injustices sustainably; or in a way that only unravels them with the short-term throwing of babies out with bath water - á la heedless violence and ideological pipe dreams. Nevertheless there is still a problem in what can look like perpetual doubting and performative questions rather than actionable assertions - of tone and posture while Rome burns before real amendments. One needs the balance between reasonable self-contemplation and action that isn't ineffective or counter-productive.

It may be of some relief that nothing is so dominant in culture as it once was - now so diffused and unfocused - in ideas as there seemed to be in past centuries, where ideas would have stake and direction but be horrifically acted on and applied, but now what does have a stake but some tepid lack of direction or soulless consumerism? A previous intellectual elitism, however reproachful, is gone; now impossible, as the tools of a culture have exceeded new boundaries. Few are good at predicting the future. People may deserve this ability to speak so very widely and excessively, I am one of these suffering people, and in assessing the swamp of modernity I cannot be a patronising voice. But the age of old media and the voices it provided did have a slim goodness, one may say, in how it was constricted and delimited. Even then there were our well known and well-written upon cultural homogenisations and those plenteous causes of alienation. Now? A sad truth is that one is often more motivated by things rarely heard than a ubiquitous call of injustice heard every day by every outlet. That bores you. Our abundance of life, again, causes some paralysis.

Democratisation of media and the free rein of anyone would not clarify anything, nor make good the maddening crowd, and so especially in an exponentially growing world that needs to be quieter if it were to be even temporarily understood; if we would need to do that anyway. Let's not get started on the faux-revolutionary hopes of *accelerationism*. There's no stopping, so it will hasten into nothing or doom, not realising what it is doing; no self-awareness, no reprieve, bereft of its institutions.

Replaying the above, the old world was no better in quality - its voices were just as terrible and in times just as pleasant - but it had less quantity and that meant something different. This quaint elitism, the confines of media and communicative channels, meant that what was distasteful was at least corralled by established limitations - its remits. Opened, and we have a rough abundance. And there's no going back from it. The best hope would be to simply maintain an [intellectual] honesty with our openness. Press will be perverted by mass.

THE FAILURES OF DISCOURSE

In philosophical and political discourse there's a
climate that has likely always been present - one
where failing to show in-group membership or ratify
an abstract and even conflicting message under an
agreed name, even in the most compatible way, will
prompt pointed dismissal. It engages the fury of not
declassing to partisanship.

I cannot consign myself to strict systems. I'm not of
the right temperament for systems. And I cannot
abide schemes.

To systematise the world is to kill it. My
rough sympathy as an artist above a [technical]
philosopher or narrative partisan comes through. Not
any grand one, but one in its banal views. I do not

want to explain everything, nor could I. If you grandly calculate the world, spiritually or materially, under an encompassing and singular system, a pinnacle method, and say 'here, there is the truth', you commit yourself to a lie: ordering, narrowly, what is in all likelihood ultimately, unbreakably, nebulous and unknown to you.

This does not say that there are, then, no truths; that all views are then legitimised in the blandest way you could understand philosophical relativism. It doesn't become a straw-man of William James[xiii] (his style of multi-viewed *pragmatism*) or a crude drawing of badly and barely understood postmodern theory.

There is not, here, an absence of narratives; as proclaiming an absence of narratives is still narratological, yet there is still a wish to remove the most *certain and acting* of narratives. It is that which has the conceit of grand order, certitude and satisfaction, over doubt, over relativity, and then confidently enacts its purposes and explanations, that is far more harmful, frightening, and practical than even a self-defeating or apathetic scepticism. Of course, "...The worst are full of passionate intensity."

It has been said before: the latter [scepticism] is to be feared in its own place, but most political motives will forever, most often, present certainty in ideology as a greater terror than caution - wherever and whatever it is. This does not mean - in response - neutrality, a lack of commitment, or complacency.

There is little illusion in how this tone is often more attractive to artful sensibilities instead of political ones. An ethics of experience, only loosely translated to philosophy, is less attractive to those who want a stage to justify themselves or to definite action. It portrays a *wishy-washy* effect, as if self-doubt was not tenable, uncertain being frightens them, and it is sadly hard to fathom that as being committed and responsible even when it instead takes the impressionist's approach of seeing multiple angles, is committed to knowing things honestly and as it can by regular revisions, and takes care to not step callously into a mess it knows little about.

When and if it does take steps it will have, it hopes, the requisite understanding rather than some dim reading pretending it is more. It is the avoidance of (as the Germans say) being *inkonsequent (inconsistent)*.

As to the aforementioned *failures of discourse*, we may first reflect briefly on this author's epistemological and ethical state. Bluntly, I can recognise hypocrisies and failed attempts at intricacy in my thought; and I can see what I think is ignored in many stricter appliers of theory… which is the muddledness and mess of one's thought. To recognise first the incongruousness of yourself or the wider world is not a puerile misdirection. There is a lack of systematic workings in most thought, a lack of coherence and comprehensiveness which is still attested to as if it did exist in all spheres. The act of thinking means, again, rethinking and then re-thinking some more. As if most of our readings of theory were not shoddy as we pinned-down labels and allegiances? We name what we do not understand. As if we were not hypocrites. I fail to order myself to a *cause* easily, besides an obstinacy in the critique of ideologies aspiring to totalism. Of hard-learned restraint that isn't paralysed.

I have no true polished view to offer, I could never say that would be available or viable to me. I could not seize the world. It always slipped away. This divorce was a point of departure, using a methodical doubt, to then confusedly try to accept the mess of things.

I am weary of the world and unable to carry out the best and most conscientious of philosophical investigations. Which leave me cold anyway. The most I could ascertain would be an accord of feeling for my fellow man, and to reject so many prosaic injustices wrought by most, if not all, those colours and leagues in their most virulent anger; and, too, in their ignorant complacencies.

I cannot make history. Others will do that. I can at least say that what is pestilent exists, one can spot falsehoods if not spot the most final of *truths*, and try always to stay apart from those spoken things and take whatever minor social truths they can. The modest hero, instead of feeling the vanity of things, recognises their own inability to be and do what they wish as a course to seeing what they *can* do. Personal, meagre heroisms - a real, non-colloquial happiness that is far harder than heroism - from ordinary people out of a simple, even simplistic decency. Courage. I would dream of that.

"One of the symbols that I have used most frequently in my novels, essays, and lectures over a period of decades is a bridge that does not exist but materialises bit by bit under the feet of someone who musters the courage to step over the abyss. The bridge may never reach the other shoreline, and that far shore probably does not even exist. The evolving but never complete person on the bridge that extends only so far as his courage does, and thus never far enough, has become the hero and antihero of all of my books." - Manès Sperber, *The Unheeded Warning 1918 – 1933.*

To see or accept this lack of polish is seen as *spineless*. It is lacking conviction, some would care to say, as they prefer absolute certainty and perfect solutions (perfect ends) even if it would be dumb and dim-witted. They can't accept an unfrocked priest and will prefer even a fanatic to a reasonable doubter who changes clubs. They can't seem to have just a lightness of touch.

They want the grand plan laid out for them that wrangles all of history and actualisation beneath it, proving its end, when what is this really? This decisive stratagem... But a hopeful divination and a myth on all sides? On the want of so much definitiveness... I've never seen much cohesion even in the greatest of minds, far above me or anyone I'd be privileged to know. I'm fed up with canned dismissals among those who won't recognise themselves, of all stripes and descriptions, underneath their ideal guises.

"Objectivity is a subject's delusion that observing can be done without him. Involving objectivity is abrogating responsibility - hence its popularity." - Heinz Von Foerster.

The real progress... comes in learning you were false all along, and all alone.

This ubiquity of deluded objectivists, those so allied to absolutism, ever indulgent, cause my struggle for self-acceptance. They wear down on everyone. They stop you from being content. Where can one avoid them?

Retort: why care about what others think? This has always been easy to suggest - recurrent enough to enter cliché and eventually entering meaninglessness. I'm not sure what to reply besides that, yes, I do care what is thought. You care what is thought as that builds you as much as your own essences, as no sure intra-personal originality really exists. We are repeating ourselves again. Even with a sight of reset priorities, more important things, resigned to myself, or what I would want in the last and most ideal analysis... it is a question of somehow recanting my emotion - my own blend of irrationalism - and indeed what is real, really *real*, is irrational. Or arational. My reason built upon irrationalities. It is Pascal's note of the heart's reasons of which the mind would be ignorant; in nicer imagery. You still have lusts for things and even avowed hermits would care somewhat for the outside world. They cared enough to avoid it - and I can't be a hermit. So I have to afford some care.

How to broadly justify the point of my mindful weariness: I'll look at what I can see (as narrow as my scope is) of the nature of knowledge, of what we can say beyond basic empiric observations. That is to say, abstract thoughts, judgements on observation. Great framers of definitions reconstruct the world by their own indulgences rather than any certain outside measure. My own objection is caused by their relationship to objectivity and intersubjectivity, and how far they think they can take their weary minds. There are political ends based on those more abstract forms now made certain simply by their insistence. After being a bit too critical of our own capacities and dismissing the thoughts of heavenly possibilities, there are still stories, ones to love; human stories bound by time. We still live as what is little and precious within mere and ungoverned history, not the cosmos. The universe probably doesn't have a story. I still - at least - have the truth of humanity without ultimate meanings or calculation.

In trying to navigate, and often struggling, around rejecting one projection of human thoughtful possibility (and human practical possibility), while not reaching to supposed opposites or outside-implied positions on my own judgements, I am pressed and I become tired. So this sort of unpolishedness and lack of certainty in thought is not to dismiss something – Reason – entirely. Just as

above one doesn't reject truth. Quite the opposite...
If one is rejecting a Hegelian basis of rationalism (or
politicised Hegelianism), or the extent of the
archetypal philosopher's psychical power unaffected
by bodily ill, that is not, then, a rejection of the power
of reason and rationality. It is to take into account the
scope of reason, practically, and by what we may
really do with ourselves. I guess me labouring over
this is due to accusations that have been levelled at
me. You say you don't really approve of something
and then they say you reject all reason itself and are
the worst of anarchists.

There's an elementary place for rational
treatises and a simpler logic of everyday; tactics and
planning, organisation and argument, for sciences and
for varied procedures, and to reject reason would be
stupid. I've never done that. Far from it. But what has
been and is being spoken of is unreasonableness, not
unreason.

I don't suffer from some relativistic subjectivism or an anarchic kind of irrationalism. Be rigorous enough in the application of reason and you'll reach epistemic limits, but I'm not so fully Kierkegaardian as to go beyond reason when it cannot go any further, or leave behind logic when all grasps at it slip. Reason becomes useless, though I don't think there's much beyond it - and it is itself, as it exists, built on irreconcilable feats and necessary complacencies. There's no truly stable ground and that can obviously cause some unease. No world beyond the 'aesthetic' is hard to accept and dissatisfying. But I can only cope with it, and to show more of what is unreasonable... we see wider abstractions rarely translate fluidly to lived-in philosophies of-the-day. Nor do quotes and inspirational posters perform as well.

We may have logics and rationales to conduct ourselves or to overcome this contention of modernity, *more and more*, of feeling lost, etc. Yet how clearly these are implemented is variable, perpetually variable, where real reason goes amiss, and I have no sound measure for how I am more of impulses than I am of strictness. There's little endorsement for this reflexiveness, but an observation of its strength above my intellect.

With this thought of irrationality it is bemusing that I'd be occupied with others who will, in the last analysis, be impervious to argument and have already and for the most part made up their minds. But that would be a reasonable position, realising a type of futility, and I'm again not *so* reasonable. So what could one's capacity for reason and discussion properly be applied to? If you're in the applying mood...

*

For ease, let's try to be more specific with my examples. In the past I have suffered from an intemperateness of tone. Maybe not in writing, as tone is harder to define and I am far more eloquent in writing, but in discourse *per se* and how I would act and carry myself.

I have the audacity to think I have matured a bit, so what does this mean for *tone* in how one wishes to reasonably convey something of yourself - or in trying to get something across to someone? I also have my own propaganda to show.

In the tone of disapproval for people's ideas a lot is said that would not merit conversion to better positions - or establish understanding for anyone involved. This is more my aversion to debate in its inadequacy. As has been repeated, I can abhor the results of intelligible certainties, of many a definition - but the stylistic choices in how to express dismissals

91

often only appeal, correctively, to those already akin to your own position, your own choir, or those on the fence - and would only make the targets of your scorn indignant. Targets of reproach need harder demonstrations to be *converted*, if you even have the influence to do that. The more vapid types of protest against various injustices work similarly (in not realising how their tone works against themselves) where the fever and hysteria of one's comprehensible and understandable suffering negates practical, real measures to overcome or remedy an unjust authority in prosperity.

The inadequacy of debate and discourse can lead the committed to perilous cliffs. I can give yet another example of this harmful sentiment, which also shows my bias against ideas still sadly extant (despite how comforted we otherwise seem). They show the failures of a common discourse.

There is a basic and reasonable position: the spirit of rebellion can reveal the evident. It can reveal solidarity with the oppressed and the imperatives of sympathy. Revolutionaries of history, of the most violent varieties, then betray this spirit in their firm convictions of working for an idealised history. Convinced so certainly of their goals they can become, like those powers before them, with clear consciences, tyrants and oppressors.

This is an easy thing to say. It has been said enough. There is often little fruitful discussion with these zealous people, and they express the failure of protest in brutal form - when instead we would want to protest well. Where their arguments failed, they took up arms and shot themselves too.

It is maybe a relief that many would-be terrorists can recant their actions at the last minute, even after extensive planning, as they search themselves and ask their God if they really need to do this. That one last doubt dawning on them with the brutality of what they must do, that would offend their own sensibilities hitherto to radicalisation, can start to dig at them. That final doubt in dogma before the most cruel and needless of acts can redeem them. It may be of some bemusement that even radical Islamists could be, at that extreme, more shaken to doubt and to find another path - or a more peaceful one within their existing frame - than the comfortable bourgeois set firm in their attractions listing Marxist quotidian, or their support for the Tory party...

There is a binary perception of a pure, untied political opposition to something seen as equally united in its own opposed brand of fervour. From the date of its inception (our poor memories of French Revolution) real unity on any *side*, for what sides we can distinguish through some parameter, most simply as *right* or *left*, was always betrayed by ringing hollow; a shallow account for anything.

Unity was always rare as one side always had ten other fissures - and to dismiss a framework would not mean you were tied to one or two positions or did not accept at least the most basic agreed terms of a dichotomy pertaining to particular places - if not universally. Frameworks, especially political, inadequate graphs and spectrum diagrams outmoded for decades yet still routinely attested to can be dismissed while standing in any corner. There are always contradictions to note in one's philosophical and political subscriptions, and in what one is named as externally. Linguistic confusion finds itself most abundant when discourse is explicitly political. The history of our political vocabulary shows gross misappropriation and feeble cataloguing, but for fear of repeating myself, or Aron, Koestler, et al (re: various sources on the datedness of political measurements), I'll quieten on the point of rejecting many definitions and wishing to teach differences.

Today's world has shown a sustained appetite for violent or grossly obstinate ideologies (whether capitalist, fascist, or communist), or for the fervour of violent overthrow at all costs, even if without the influence of previous generations, convinced too that any co-operation or intermediation means death. It shows as well an equally sustained appetite for powers to remain even if they are cruel. We never got a *post-ideological* turn.

There is on many a side seeking their goals an absolute damning of individuals when one still needs imperfect allies; as you are thoroughly incapable by yourself. The world for them is still Manichean rather than confusing, multifarious and diffused; and they see themselves in their consciences and their theory as almost perfect or obvious, when the world and what answers we can have are not perfect and neither always obvious. How does one have a nuanced reciprocity with minds that are so fanatically partisan?

There are opposing extremes that perform the same acts of dethronement for different ends. Can one bother to discuss such things with either *totalitarian twin*? Can you convince Lysenkoists?[xiv] Is this medicine for the dead?

With this, these thankfully moribund but nonetheless vocal personalities, revolutionary or counter-revolutionary, often unfortunately excuse any pragmatic or far-extending chance - a chance at remedying the ills they see by slow increment and preserving themselves, monument, justice, their own legitimacy, and life; if they would want to do that anyway, which many seem not to be so interested in.

Destruction at any cost for a prophetic end, one that is not possible, excuses useful creation, the truer possibilities of any slow modification, or real sustainability. Nor is a reserved, old establishment

really a sustainable or stable locus. Short-term battle
may merit arms, as we don't have here the resigned
refusal to fight things, but the long drag of
ideological fare doesn't warrant unfettered barbarism,
random anger, wanton death and all of one's violent,
forceful means.

Is this battle against fanatical ideas, against
ideology, opposing but similarly barbaric schemes
not as moribund as they'd be now, that of the last
century? Are we, in a very simple use of the phrase,
as some say, simply in some new post-ideological
era? Perhaps battles in the new arena of politics and
war - that I won't hope to pertinently and correctly
dissect - don't have these same historical stakes; the
press of *Cold War*, the awful struggle of interwar and
postwar crimes, Hitlereans and certified Stalinists (or
both their *fellow travellers* and other respective,
assorted attendants)… today's atmosphere is seen as
cloudier and has its histories based on newer varieties

of grudge, different techno-cultural hallmarks, with men and women and others who breathe different air... and only the foolhardy will say with such sure and definitive tones what the state of the union is. Contesting emptily, faltering in assertion, ideals of justice pursued with stupid ideas, it seems that lots of voices - even if these voices are confined to shouting at walls - would still be afraid of admitting their intellectual insecurity (one I must honestly admit but try not to flaunt or patronise with), they offer to the world their certain solitude but with sad condescension, and are reluctant to present their diagnosis of world affairs, themselves, the direction of history, or a study of past influences... as *unsure*.

Those who could really give a good and detailed account of history or sociological directions, military rationales, cultural grievances, are likely and more often quieter, subtler, obscure and reserved sorts who in pronouncing conclusions or reviews of the world - its items we are paralysed with - will inevitably be shaded and noting of the varied complications of analysis.

Rather than have Ockham's razor, those hearing these notes from the rarer and closeted, and not receiving the simplest of headline answers, will prefer the vivisection of Ockham's chainsaw. Not a simpler world, but a simplistic one. The review that so many are eager for both in the editorial office and in comfortable living rooms: an answer.

A column must surmise all the world, everything must be said, as it is wished. A summary is reacted to so fiercely and confidently by so many typists of all different descriptions that one becomes upset as they are simultaneously suspicious. For a moderation these people are surely capable of in the cases of their private activities disappears when faced with anything without them. Moral outrage is easy - and true moralism is hard.

One could robustly call all of these efforts, simply, if reservedly, intellectual dishonesty. No matter creed or allegiance.

The above and the earnest desire for the easiest ordering of things seems to manifest in all times, in its varying ways, as a lack of particular modesty while feigning weariness; lacking a wiser maturity, and not holding a sincerity with one's limitations.

The nucleus of this straightforward, simplified divining of basic order has its worst reflections in all of our multiple radicalisms. If I was more studious and far less lazy or fatigued, I'd invoke Miguel de Unamuno and his Ethic of Doubt[xv].

How we forge our justifications and the basis of an ethic, more prudently on a lack of dogmatic ground, reflects the honesty we would wish for in striving for good discourse, quality thinking, and remaining just while living in the ontological unknown. It is not pallid scepticism stuck in its own contesting, or contention, but the astute and forwarding use of possible nihilism (in a rejection of it that doesn't forget its ground), seeing the problems of scepticism, and using itself to work around them while not forgetting the importance of that doubt in curbing cocksure thought and vanity.

We are often those not knowing why we would go about a romp or knowing why we act at all, and we readily live within the impositions of our forged motives. There's likely motive we can see without us, but that's harder and takes more effort to really confront and deal with. It takes more experience to see than I have.

In a last analysis, we have passionate minds that misuse passion. They don't practice a particular moderation, nor temper moderation itself, and in their anger they shift the cruelties of the world while not seeing where it would be going or what it is becoming. Inward conduct has tendencies to root its way into the more egregious examples of partisan action; and no matter on which periphery these inquisitions happen, those wishing to persist in intellective consistency and a lack of dishonesty, maintaining the elimination of lies (where *'truth'* is a fishy thing), may do better if they can step back slightly to consider what anyone and themselves are really doing. Practice Wou-Wei, even; my meagre wish is simply to have myself, or others that would bother me, to conduct themselves honestly with the difficulties of intellectual responsibility before they take steps carelessly. Truth won't be reached by jumping off the cliff.

A saving grace as much as it is a bane - considering the abundance of active and motivated ideas towards drastic measure - would be the willingness of most to live calmly, in querulous gratification, despite the injustices upon them. This pains me, as there's no wish to keep-up the particular conservatisms that propagate all the usual social injustices, where our current violence is just as awful as one that wishes to change things over upholding the unjust (and I have no time for the Right). But considering the brutality of death I have had to restrain my stimulating dreams for change that is called for with pressing emotion, and realise the debt and costs of usurpation that would be beyond me. The mollification (mitigation) of injustice should come before a staunch and awkward march to an idealised revolution, and especially one founded on false sciences.

Today's victims as tomorrow's executioners is obvious, a banal objection, yet the *realistic* and *practical* minds, wanting captive minds and futures, opposed to being morally condemned, see who has discredited them as, at best, detached from reality and from supposed *vital interests*. In a better light the *moral side* is seen more admirably as literary, maybe artful, yet still it is denigrated as some vague humanism somehow abandoning the necessary harshness of real politics. It would not occur to these *so realistic* of men that even airy, fluttery words could actually represent unwavering stands, against a struggle that never succeeds; too against standing oppressors, nor that their own position is founded really on prejudices, nor in truth, and attractions to prophecy and myth rather than actual realisms.

Little is done, physically, maybe, when one isn't murdering all the pets and relatives of an awful leadership: but what is *done* with replacement? Does this succeed in its most famous forms? Has one only, actually, betrayed real defiance for a lofty cause out of any reach? In murders worse than the previous Tzars? I feel banal in saying this, as if it were all said and done and I am just a parrot.

One is not resigned to the unjustifiable if they forget to murder people.

You are still intransigent against what is terrible, you still don't allow it a discourse, when you must you still prepare for war, and when the most important of change is possible... it is best worth doing if one has the tact, resources, prescience and responsibility which would help one to do it correctly. Rather than do something so impatiently only to have a harder long-run - a perpetual *agon* unresolved. Risks can be necessary. Removing the lulls of bureaucracy or fuddled heads in show business, fostering innovations, requires taking risks. But that is different to the *risks*, which are more political crimes than they are of taking reasonable chances, preached by ideologues. Many of those indignant orders of violence are called for in the name of idealising rather than a primary feeling of desperation or a way of real progress. The risks wonted from outsiders to

106

an experience seeking rectification are often different to the risks wanted by those really living within something (re: the ideas of many intellectuals and militants compared to their *subjects*, everyday working people; etc.).

Most cannot enact sweeping change. I likely cannot in any great way change minds or force movements. I do hope at least that some bright spark would bring about more attentive work in facing environmental woe. Besides that (an issue perhaps more pressing), if I could *force* movements I would still not remove the indigence of powers reinforced by my fervency and destruction of random properties - if I were able to go down that route of less efficient protest. Our opponents are stronger than we think and we need to act tactically and more astutely. Things need destroying? It seems rather unrelated to truly changing ideas, especially in founding any prosperity to one's plan, or creation (our more effective dignity).

Benign institutions need a long history to help engender their quintessence and reason for existing. We cannot make new lives overnight.

There is no doubt that things need to be reformed, changed, demolished or upended; and destruction is an easy way, it seems, to beget rapid change. But it is a change that is not often properly targeted, tactful, or one with much foresight into how it may preserve a greater quality of life. Destruction can be romantically attractive and have its own place - and it surely does have some place when the time is right - but it is something that needs to be mediated if it is to be worth it. Despite its aesthetics, destruction is not often so radical. It quickly becomes reckless and distracted. It will, often and inevitably, become just as corrupt, misguided, and abusive as a cruel power already in place. What we want instead, abstractly, is a path to real change that would last. I should make clear that I am not objecting to riotous reactions to prosaic injustices – or the righteous anger held against racial injustice. Which I share. Rather, there is an objection to developed ideology (from a variety of political extremes, often opposing) that takes the idea of destruction somewhere else, in an imperceptive way, and not fortuitously.

Places with history have felt within them all that has been said within, and cannot easily be replaced. Sense Miłosz's peculiar dissatisfaction with a desert California compared to an expansive Lithuanian history...[xvi] It takes some time to live. Life needs to be thought on. Nor is much that is artful really done under that which cannot create new things after a fiery disposal.

A truer rebellion has a paradox. It needs order. It should not reinstate what is terrible. A politics, not new, of *limits* against injustice. Mediation. Against those most desperate of transgressions. The most rampant type of demolition (of old orders) also works against the idea of bourgeoning support for most causes, as one's only respect will be through fear: and there's little worse respect than that. Nor is it lasting.

Imagine leaving only charcoal to defend... You forget... that revolution has always been an illusion. Especially in our history. There are detestable powers, things need to be removed, and renovated, but how are you to really mend the world? As if you could?

"To make a good omelette it is not enough to break thousands of eggs, and the value of a cook is not judged, I believe, by the number of broken eggshells. If the artistic cooks of our time upset more baskets of eggs than they intended, the omelette of civilisation may never again come out right, and art may never resuscitate. Barbarism is never temporary." - Albert Camus, *Create Dangerously*, lecture on December 14, 1957 at the University of Uppsala in Sweden.

Razing the ground so impatiently does not give you a pristine opportunity to rebuild, because most are frankly incapable of that. The actors have little consistency, time, cleverness or resource. No time to cover the interval between myth and reality and neither any moral high ground. There is no real idea of how to enact replacements for regimes, and more commonly in those states of absolute disposal a void of power and a scramble by anxious and enthused souls with little wisdom or intelligence. Not even some sort of social history is on their side, where they are helping the governance of moral history, a narrative progress, and that their impositions would somehow be justified by it...

"The so-called dialectic of social history results from the transformation of reality into an idea. Each régime is sharply defined, and a unique principle is ascribed to it: the principle of capitalism is opposed to that of feudalism or that of socialism. Finally, it is suggested that régimes are contradictory and that the transition from one to another is comparable to the transition from thesis to antithesis. This is to commit a double error.

Régimes are different and not contradictory, and the so-called intermediary forms are more frequent and more durable than the pure forms. Supposing the principle of capitalism to be connected to feudalism as 'nothingness' is to 'being' or Spinozism to Cartesianism, there is nothing to guarantee that the accidental determinism will fulfil this intelligible necessity. Supposing that socialism reconciles feudalism and capitalism as 'becoming' reconciles 'being' and 'nothingness', the advent of the synthesis is not predictable in the same way as a nuclear explosion or the trade cycle.

On the plane of events there is no automatic selection which conforms with our moral requirements." –

Raymond Aron, *The Opium of The Intellectuals*.

Without real justification for what one would fancifully wish to impose, there's no rationalistic nor ethical backing for those abrupt ideologies that betray revolt; caliphate, counter-revolutionary romanticism or revolutionary rationalism, the *end of history...*

Sad experience has inoculated me against wanton death or extreme for any cause, cause unjustified nor achievable by fair standards, and most *causes* of that so historic ilk are dreams - more nightmares - promising much and delivering little. Social causes worth dying for are not so vindictive. One should not accept definite models and utopias, and neither be seduced by parables. The faked universality of one's vocation… Leave alone so many abstractions. We don't have those heavens.

To use Sperber's phrase: "Mark this carefully: we stormed heaven not that we might live there but to show all mankind, *ad oculis*, that heaven is empty."

A hard message to accept without resignation.

In the need for change people can do better than dreams. There are enough dreamers in the world to call for necessary change, but there are few reasonable people to guide us in a practicable direction in an imperfect world with imperfect means: the only means and answers available to us being imperfect. These ideologies of perfection were always contrary to psychology, to real interests. Always working against better interests. Prosperity may, with some hope, frown upon those writers and artists so absorbed by their agony that they sought solace and uplift through a spiritual '*cure*', a *cure* in cool diagnosis, in historical prophecy, rather than having their anguish made live, dramatically, as a show for future generations in deliberation. Change happens, change is needed, renovation is possible, but when it is real it is slow; or if not it is better planned and calculated by tactical insidiousness. Greater minds than I have far better exposed the self-subversion of fanatical devotion and a reaction to authority that is frenetic and untamed.

*

I've maintained already that most (those who would do better being convinced of something else from what they already hold so passionately) will still be impervious to argument, but for what can be done to create a sympathy in one's opposition for your own position, or to convince the undecided (if you must

115

go about convincing people of things), anger works less well than would often be thought. It can at least name an injustice, but at its furthest reaches it begets disorder and not changed convictions. I am never very angry, in the conventional sense, at those most massive of political horrors. I am thoroughly upset by them. To be focused and upset works differently from an unfocused anger. Anger can be fine for a while, but it cannot last forever if we want to be prosperous. And it soon becomes - banally – poisonous to the self.

I would have to learn a sense of understanding for how something adverse, even horrific, can come about in our minds and in our practices if I want to accurately face it.
Most fail at giving even a proper label to a rival with such a poor grasp of political vocabulary. If I cannot grasp what and how my opposition is, and academically consider their own logic - however

primitive it is - then I have little possibility in being able to resolutely and justifiably condemn them. I may want more privacy, now, than to readily engage myself against the incorrect, and it stands that I cannot kill or convert the incorrect. The only chance or possibility available to me is to maybe stop others, friends, from falling into traps by finding them early. Insofar as one's rival hasn't reached a limit of no return from their darkness, discourse with someone you can still maintain hope for needs to be done with a higher standard, by a legitimacy, if it is to be done at all.

There are some patent evils, puerile evils, from which many cannot be recovered.

As such I find little reason to shout at them, and measures to counter such fanaticism are things I am not, physically, able to take part in whatever my wishes besides merely slighting them. I then have the privilege to live quietly. I am so tired of argument

against what is obviously dark and monstrous, at
pointing out the same references again and again
against something that will not listen anyway.
I give up on the fanatics.

In argumentation, anyway, I should be more
prudent if I would want to convince one of anything
(especially partisan) beyond briefly moving someone
by impulse and responses. There are deeper motives
applied to violence, no care for argument in any case,
and a want to raze things totally as they are so unjust.

I can only suggest that there are no best
choices, no definitive solutions, and only the next
best thing. The least bad thing. To scrap everything
so thoroughly doesn't mean anything good will come
out of the waste, and history seems to vindicate me
(or those others who would say the same far better
than I).

Those most moved by outbursts will already
be aligned with you; where any real threat

considering changing itself and in deeper

understandings would not be moved by your passion,

reflexively irked by your rudeness, and instead, if at

all, moved only by something clear and which they

could comprehend according to their own

sympathies. It means to be insidious if you really

wish to *convince*.

I think this gives a clearer view of what my priorities

should be...

PEOPLE OF RESPONSIBILITY

I have a hard time accepting my world with its setting
of priorities: with a lack of quiet space despite myself
as a loud person who would still find some verve in
curious conversations. Self-acceptance, if not
actualisation, means coping with what is external too,
and unfortunately it is hard to always live at an
uncaring remove from the world even if it would be
tempting to. I am repeating myself. Despite what the
meditative may wish to say... you cannot forget the
world very easily, and to be engaged with the world
means something nuanced, a shaded expression, for
which we require different depths to our discourse.

It is hard to express this illustration of
myself directly; without being circumlocutory. It

amounts to tracing entirely a history of personal thought that would be beyond my capability to reflect. I want to show my love for people and their impetus for my growth, the hard-learned direction of my reading and evaluation of ideas, but I cannot spell-out the biographies of people in pedantic detail. The purpose of this section would simply be 'here, these are people I like. I like what they say', as a reflection of interest. Which is cheap, but my expedience may be justified with further reading. John Ruskin wrote in Exercise VI of his *The Elements of Drawing*, in his guidance of how to draw a tree... "Do not take any trouble about the little twigs, which look like a confused network or mist; leave them out, drawing only the main branches as far as you can see them distinctly." As such, I don't feel the need to focus intently on too many twigs.

*

I covet an idea of responsibility - one which is mistaken (and has been shown to be linguistically mistaken in other tongues) with a type of full engagement, purest ideology, at any cost: with action but not with consideration, nor deliberation. There's the import to speak on demand, to be (somehow categorically) a general intellect rather than - preferably - a discrete intellect. There are caustic ambitions held above the thought of not crossing certain lines, and a need for things so powerfully that it becomes all well and fine to endorse certain crimes. I need something against that. I shout: No. With no restrictions there is an unlimited slavery.

The rebel who says no is not simply a bland proposition, solely of fighting the quo; kicking against the pricks, the bastards... the spirit of that still holds ground, but to say no in this way is also a rejection of moral apathy and of the brutality of political realisms - in their respective reactions to egregious atrocity, or meaninglessness. I have my own reactions to similar premises. It is a rejection and revulsion to becoming a similar face to a prick, or tyrant. And the furthest mark, harder to articulate well and harder to grasp with a rational head... is this rejection held concurrently against a vacant countenance, an indifference that this defective outside world has. To hold upstanding morale without faking, without pretending, that it has stable grounds and solid building foundations. Even if it invokes and uses old ways. One can use the good of a God without God, one can see void and not do everything. Our world hitherto was not as solid as we pretended.

We can pluck morale almost from nothing, snubbing mystic or rational bases that wear some mask of certitude conjured to feel grounded, and that is hard to live and behave by. Many find it hard to justify, if we need to do that. There is a defence: if one founded all their behaviour so consciously on a dogmatism that was now broken, that they did not sin due to the fear of Hell, it is to the honour and benefit of the human species that among us are those who would not be so defiantly bound to solid bases. Those who are tied to ideas so ferociously cannot easily act like undaunted stoics in a new world of shattered atoms. That most do not desist from good action when they cease to believe in old things - in formulae - (as is this impulsiveness of us) is to some advantage. One can count that people will invent new reasons; the stuff beneath ideas, the awkward steps of rationale, will save them. If one had instead held so firmly to firmest dogma, the dismantling of previous orders shows a great sense of loss for these poor souls. The reflexive can be more advantageous, and nor are they so anarchic or unprincipled. Virtue is not based on dogma, but dogma upon virtue. The better sorts can hold firm and create.

Holding this responsibility in front of those dilemmas, against the actively violent, against fanaticism, is pressing on the heart. It can become a madness. In other words it is a rejection of certain metaphysical notions used more broadly than they could be. Notions used as epistemic justifications of societal ends. A rejection that would seem trite, even... If I lay some small authority to Wittgenstein (forgetting his epistemological wild goose chase) I may at least place myself under his monument[xvii]. Holding that [certain rejections] while sitting in surroundings that feel these effects are out-of-fashion, while it kneels to shifts in trends it fails to dissect, is a trial and a chore. They would forget the fogginess of motivations.

*

On the use of principles: I am stunted and humbled by those many varied, intelligent sorts I can admire while I disagree with them. There are far more eloquent Gaullists, as well as communists and *communisants*, a conventional West or those of other disparate and opposed ideals than I... that will forever be of an openness and creativity above my own restricted self. And as is shown I dilly-dally between people in my condemnations. Yet scrupulous thought and large capabilities, intelligibility, while fostering a knowledge or accumulation of attendant information, can and will lack wisdom or intuitions.

Polyglots and professors will still be subject to moral darkness, they can still commit rape and murder, and so what conclusion am I making from this?

I think, at least, that rigour and semantic purism can be, or should be, secondary to morality or

humility. Not that it is unimportant to be rigorous -
certainly not - but that we need to be studious in a
better [or the correct] way. Or otherwise that there are
many, of all descriptions, who pretend to have rigour
as an excuse for an impoverished morality - or
stunted emotional growth. I'll reject those who
"...learn to predict a fire with unerring precision.
Then burn the house down to fulfil the prediction."[xviii]

Some modern sophists, of the last century
and now, demand a reduction of feeling and
conscience in the name of what they think is a greater
intelligibility. They want to order the murky No
Man's Land of decisions, bad results with good
intention, good done by doing shit, or a banality to
reasons for action... under an insular cause; they
want to be simply and consequentially ordered. Men
of great integrity still commit crimes. They'll react to
evils by exacerbating them. They augment injustice -
showing anger rather than, more simply, upset and

clearer courses for antidote besides wild outrage. An alienated madness and not a countenance, facing an expression: that what is best is mostly impossible. They'll reject such rough moralising as useless and impractical as they ordain, by dirty means; practice that does not redeem us from *agon* by any long or short term.

So practical, so efficient, so easily hoisted with their own petard.

*

How could I further stress and illustrate this responsibility I want, a particular one, by peopled example? I do not embolden myself by most easily identifiable means. That can be pretentious, as I require some explanation of all these things that I am rejecting and those few I share something with - in spirit (intellectively if not by familial association).

128

But in comparison to many others explaining themselves I am not dense nor opaque with what and who I identify my character with. I just wish to take some care with it; because you say you are one thing and are connoted quickly and instantly with a perceived opposition, and I am a weaselly man who cannot abide that bluntness. I would think it callous and shallow to be able to say what you are so comfortably - picking some available preset body from the comic store and staying 'yes, this commodity is me'. Easy self-description doesn't portray much depth, and is often a scary sight in those so acting and certain in their opinions. It is always some on-going, rethinking process that accords my self-description. And I am still left unsure of it. A stranger to thyself.

Rather than write some complicated treatise, which would take more time and patience than I have, I will substantiate myself anxiously and attest to the authority of past intellects. I can claim some complimentary allegiance to a list of people to shine on my weary conduct. There's a feebleness to it but also a necessary convenience. As if our own worth was not also found in the roles of others? You write to yourself in the mirror of others, if I need yet another reason to attest to others. What was secondary could not be relinquished from my throat. This is the use of intellectual history. There are people who in their way, in their time, were preoccupied with a century of crimes. They are perhaps the best examples (as men and women of letters) of those who did not fall to violent decadence, though neither did they fall to any absent pacifism - with qualities of honesty reflecting the better judgements available of their times.

A list chosen, too, for political and indeed passionate reasons: Hannah Arendt, Raymond Aron, Albert Camus, René Char, Jean Grenier, Arthur

Koestler, Czesław Miłosz, George Orwell, Boris Pasternak, Ignazio Silone, Manès Sperber, Simone Weil...[xix] Let's not write out a litany of biographies but grasp at the crux of my adherence.

All these people held something similarly, politically or morally, while with their more obvious differences that go without saying... The commonality of these late writers, some of whom have brought me the greatest joy, those shadows of known-people if not heroes, was an awareness of our burdens and an antidote to overreactions, as well as under-reactions, against moral and political confrontations seen on almost any side of the landscape.

One should not, still, appropriate their witness but merely disseminate them. There is a moral or civic need to bring the suffering experiences of those from the past into the present, for reasons of awareness, rather than subsuming individual suffering into one's own contemporary, party goals under narratives of progress and systematised history. I am not so much an *écrivain engagé* with my writing commitments, though my reasons for dissemination are not just personally therapeutic. I am stuck between a desired practice of self-soothing quietism and the public need for the artist.

Why do I need a list of people? Is it not a pallid thing, almost lifeless, without such detail and pattern to really speak of a theory of things? I am not here for that. I cannot comprehend or give anyone theory. In any comprehensive way, at least. I am short, and when I speak of these people I do not do so blandly.

These people… they are not just a recent history of grim events and advances.

I have always wanted people, even strangers, the sensual world and the unwomanly face of war to give me my personal history. This is a history of idea and social biography, of scents and touches. I could not have my measly excuse for history just as some list of events and purposes. I need the words of men and women who I could know intimately. To see the faults of our historical players in context.

To situate these aforesaid people more specifically, in their experience, my wish is for an illustration of those more unorthodox members of Resistance, additionally, [Jacques Ellul[xx], et al] who remained as voices of conscience while they were swamped from all angles by a want of unfettered vengeance that turned-in on itself, and a Cold War variety of materialism and polarity. Consumerism, and the proposed antithesis likewise. The difficulty of this political standing in that time, untied to this or that simpler loyalty, represents an admirable philosophical persuasion I can dream to imitate.

Others, such as Jean-Paul Sartre - still an open and creative intellect - enjoyed a greater influence, yet in the merry company of fellow travellers 'dispensed absinthe morality' through the Left Bank and a revolutionary spirit of the times that often thought in bland binaries, and betrayed true revolt. They were monologists and polemicists that were not self-doubting. They were far too sure of what they had misread. The vices of capital, the ding of the cash register, still accompanied their contrary sentiments and defiant ideas.

These aforesaid outliers represented those intellectuals who did not lose their way during the mid-20th century to either fascist extremes, tribal nationalisms, communism, or plain self-importance and in so doing courted unpopularity and isolation. Their failure to ratify an easy in-group membership caused them some grief - attacks from all sides and even from supposed friends. Though regardless of that they were neither retreated, isolated aesthetes. To be engaged in French and European politics is given a higher place of importance in long tradition, the feedback of 1789, and as a recent intellectual history those particular people, remaining independent and responsible, presented a warning to those close to them about how they could stray too far. There is political engagement, and then there is responsible, informed engagement.

I choose these people carefully, for I could recite a dumb number of literary figures to consume and emulate, and as representations, but am here picking a certain moral to the story. They represented a type of confrontation to recent events vindicated more so in later years than in their present settings. Again, they are intimate people for me even from their distance in time.

I also have an indebtedness to the late Tony Judt[xxi], who helped further rouse in me this engrossed appreciation of a recent history of ideas. A history of causes. As something specific, beyond a broader philosophical investigation, not in abstractions, I became enamoured with these acclaimed outsiders of the last century and sensed a nervous proximity to them, an accordance, in part with tinted-glasses (as I could romanticise an already mythologised era), yet too with finding a type of studied devotion to individuals that was applicable, pragmatic, and tangible to my life and actions unlike so many theorists I was bent towards otherwise.

Who I choose most carefully to disseminate, recommend, and repeat in my own breaths somehow, by my own way of thinking, has a confused course when I still want to be agreed with it. I want to diagnose it but not do so coolly. I am less drawn, with exceptions, to what could be called 'philosophical tract' from *Anglophone* sources even though I would be forced to encounter those sources by living with them - for a preference that is not well illuminated. If it somehow could be…

I still took Beckett's quietism, and minimalism, as something important and to perhaps embody, and prefer some poetry and novels from my home (Dickens, Forster, Larkin, Orwell - and indeed it is in my native tongue; of course I will find it easier), but these are mostly easy exceptions and as a summation of more poignant sentimental attraction, of philosophy formally (of my more active influences), I was drawn further to a continent with certain exiled, less popular persons who fought against something, against many things, and who were later exonerated by turns in events (the testimonies of Solzhenitsyn, Leszek Kołakowski[xxii], etc). It was with a specific interwar and postwar history of ideas, its biography written by figures arrestingly opposed to many different oppositions, that in which I saw, mostly, my peculiar fancy. It were as if these people were part of a reasonable fable. I couldn't pretend, as so many would, to be isolated on my island only separated by 20 miles of sea from land it is still long intertwined with.

My most favourite works were almost always foreign, *La Peste* made me weepy, and I would guess that this allowed me to appreciate those distant others as much as those in my immediate geographical proximity. I would still be suspicious of those who'd dislike their own soil too much, in favour of another, but that's already been said. My attachment to English literature and language does not need to be justified. It just is. I live it as it is identified in my being, the place where I have had my growth and physical experiences.

Is my solidarity, then, with wider European sources not so much organic but intellectual? Maybe it is both, if I could be so viscerally affected by lands I am unknown to, holding no direct ancestry to my knowledge; and even if there was that... I have never cared too much for familial history and more for myself in my present, selfishly; I always feared ancestry because of its misuse and preferred worldly ideas to old parochial allegiances. But I'm unable to be so cultured and worldly by my own impediments. Places still alien to me, places I will never be able to visit, brought me more joy than a village just because I lived there. It could be guessed that a projection of love onto a foreign entity made up for the inadequacies of what was immediate to me. But as has been said in a previous section I cannot hate old England so much, and that sneering at your history starts to hurt you. You can accept it for what it is and enjoy its smaller items of interest.

In any event this solidarity is preferential, shaking one's hand across the sea, and not something tinged with a supernatural history, reserved for believers, that I cannot access. I have no love for nationalism, though I cannot claim a wanted spirit of universal cosmopolitanism either. Frontiers do exist, but are at least temporary. I was ascribed the literature of my own milieu simply from being there, tied to it, no matter my reservations and despite the strength of my individualism. I attained an idea of my own identity from people elsewhere after simply looking, and with the longer process of characterisation and rethinking.

This, those people, and the sore questions that are posed, gives me a disorganised thesis of responsibility. A shadow of a theory. It won't so soon replace old narratives or fix a new mess, but it may as well help me. It shows those who, in the eyes of this little author, would be best to emulate and have as mindful friends. We can grow from their outside aid. A haphazard growth of contrarian rejections, valuable assertions, and pity, gave me these varied and idealised inspirations both specific as well as eclectic.

I have worth inside other things, but I should take care not to misprint those things.

These figures are chosen, studiously too, as I said once that I value modern voices more than ancient ones, but this has some nebulous depth that would be missed.

I can read the ancients and there is some flavour, but I have more sympathy for people closer to me, by time, by culture, from shared activities, and by the undeniable element of modern celebrity idol I cannot really challenge. It means that by biographical detail these men and women lived in a time still in living memory and can maybe better serve, as closer to us, our modern functions and kinships. Or mine.

One cannot so surely pluck from history Epicurus or Aurelius and functionally apply them. I appreciate them, but too I have other opinions that may be unjustifiable. Indeed, many are frozen in their time and place. Their concerns are, in parts, no more;

and we can only extract their reasoning and experience insofar as we understand what they were dealing with in their time. There is only so much timelessness to principle and we have a temporal priority.

Maybe I react to something too? To ugly dismissals of people without reading and the suspiciousness of the canon... Even the last century has moved quickly. I may be trying to indulgently describe a liking of something I need not have to explain. It is just important that I like something.

I needed voices who are closer to me. Warnings and ways of coping with my own stock. It is probably far-fetched to expect modern politics to take Montaigne or Tocqueville (though not as a colonialist) as primary driving influences cited directly in manifestos and policy, and cynically I find little use for philosophers as political participants, most of whom invariably 'fall down the well'.

Individual growth may be the more prudent course, but again I cannot be so easy with where I stake my claims and my action. These listed persons did well at least, committed well, and I see a modern nobility, warts and all, that is still humbled and measured.

*

With my temperament I am hypocritically reserved, in fragile conflict, to armchair politics; with a question of personal consciences over and above the rules of the party where I can have no leverage or face. I'm giving words rather than actions. My actions become, with or without my wishes, confined to myself.

Public intellect, activist, distraught over public emergencies while confident and comfortable in private arenas; I am not. I'd be far more conscious or preoccupied with an individual and personal

143

morality over the finer details of politicking, which I am not adept or constituted so well with to be cocksure in. Yet I am not a complete egoist, nor set against collectives. This is what that responsibility also shows. When we are so committed to being politically engaged, if we see politics as omnipresent and above one's person, we can forget that charity begins at home - to maintain insular respect. And we forget to question our own dogmatism. It is maybe a succession to these aforementioned people, with popularity, which is what I dreamily miss (or long for), with some pretentiousness, and which is a long-shot in the world of modern saturation. The lack of personal consciences, replaced by public ones, and the wide acts of reductionism make it harder to cajole the world to such a personal seat. My intuitive lusts are tied to high-flung and sanctimonious wants - memorialised in past figures. I don't often enjoy the conflicts of literature and it wears on my mind already worn enough. I wince at the thought of my sanctimony - in where I find interest - this literature of both cure and poison. The string of issues that impede my simple possibility for adoration, for comfort, of where I'm from, for people in basic livings, makes me wish for an unexplored life.

I want this easier comfort, both as a participant in affairs and personally, that is hindered by my discerning sights and others' corruption - where I envy these crowds and their liberty I can so rudely distaste. What type of accordance, acquiring and receipt, do I want? I will try to detail it… In trying just to sustain oneself… pathology isn't, obviously, much of a good companion for living blissfully either by physical action or by avoiding mental frictions.

Can I still live and die by what I proclaim in others?

WHY I WRITE, WHAT I WOULD WRITE

Much of my preceding bibliography had as part of its sum a maddened accounting of other people, of those whom I deemed worthy of proposing and propagating. This does too, but lately I have wanted or embraced an uneven form of collations, *literary* prose over technical intricacy, as a way to justify my lack of formal capabilities.

   With the accounting of others I knew obliquely that I had little, or nothing, new or significant to say that had not already been said, and this put me in an incapable position.

One could easily and without much of a stretch conclude that there'd be no need to write anything, at

146

least technically philosophical, and add to the clutter of an already saturated world.

All I could really say that would be commensurate of evaluation and critique will have been done in a style and class far above my capacity. At first, some years ago, this produced a lazy, ignoble effort on my part in writing with me citing too directly from sources with some brief amendment or commentary - before or after stating approval or disapproval. Biographical details, historical descriptions, these were things that I both dutifully and duplicitously decided should be borrowed and taken from other sources, with customary edits, and for some reason of marketing or free advertisement I wanted to reaffirm and restate facts as if 'for the record', while still giving the most basic credit and due, and adding my own sordid conclusions.

Why did I need to repeat in my own words something already precise?

It were as if I'd take a thesaurus and my slim ingenuity, and replay what was already said plainly and well... And a lot of authorship seems to be like this. I wrote enough of my own rubbish, though not intentionally, just sort of as one breathes, to supplement what I was fond of - and at least the experience gave practical editorial lessons that are still being learnt. I cannot regret this path so much considering the youthful drive of it (and as has been said - physical and pathological weaknesses may give one some leeway), though I do wish retrospectively that I was not so lethargic in my aim to retell particular stories. I still am now, and this book could be a lot longer than it is.

In my past I had a more rigid, seemingly common adherence to a type of positivism and literal readings of things I'd now not approve of, and if I interrogate myself I see these qualities are now highly mitigated if not fully removed. When you reread your past there's going to be obvious recoils at what you wrote. I am irritated by plain mistakes, style and syntax, but simultaneously there has to be an acceptance of the time, age, and the place I was in that fostered those words. One still scarcely knows how to write.

As well as this mentioned recording of others came a sly, suggested, though not directly expressed motive as to why and what, then, I would write had I the time or planning. The acknowledgment of this reason, or set of reasons, became better known with repetition and re-reading. While there is some air of formality and distinct subject to my oeuvre, I managed to state without a full understanding (that only came later) that these projects where therapeutic and personal exercises, excuses for prose and brief essays, wrapped in a thin cellophane of philosophical academicism. They were private journals before the idea of me as a pamphleteer. The repeated 'c.f Montaigne' finally meant something - to write 'for oneself' came to a more lucid view than a dim idea of aesthetic justification. A devoted writer should find a new start in each book, though there is an obvious referential quality to all that I am doing.

I was never good with stylistic consistency, with structure, and prone to tangential writing with a style over its substance. Seduced by bells and whistles. I still struggle to judge all but the most egregious examples of writing. In style and language itself you would be attracted more to the aesthetics of words, as you still would be, but to the negative extent of giving "solidity to pure wind", so common in philosophy, where a writer tries to sound far more profound by what words and phrases they pick. I can look back and sigh at style, but it was something to learn from. And it would be too sentimental to try and purge my vocabulary of all these new wordy additions that come with my time and reading experience. Undoubtedly the act of publishing my work became an egocentric experiment and reflection on my philosophical and literary growth, in an oddly public display, simply not confined to private journals or empty blogging.

My first attraction in text was to a type of scholasticism (a caricature of it), where I wanted to inflect my self-indulgence into a type of professionalism. This was soon realised to be some mistake and with hindsight it is more obvious, again, that everything I was doing was a personal project - writer above philosopher.

It was said in a clear way, but with some conflict, as I still retained the peculiar wish for formality despite my technique, my personality, basic editorial mistakes, eccentric structure, and I was ultimately confused and still am as to what I was doing.

I had to speak from my gut and from my flesh. To that associated, and less in wildly abstract terms. I should say definitively that I am, in essence, a hazardous diarist over anything else.

*

There is more recently in my thought and writing a latter-day occupation with moralism (not in the derisive English sense – 'to moralise' - but more in the French sense considering a long tradition of saint-like '*moralistes*', distinct from the usual *public intellectual* by their own sense of private disquiet). That is to say, to be a *moraliste* but not a *moraliser* of polarised rhetoric and violent enthusiasms... we need to make this important distinction. It is to have in some part an ambiguity most want to disavow; they want so much *engagement*, politically, and expediently, but lack the responsibility to be thoughtful or even correct, and they write a *tract* which is less favourable than showing a basic temperateness or awareness. We don't have *lessons*, here; reasons for teleological *advance* (others can give those), we have a countenance with wrongdoings and the slim possibilities available to us.

Above there has already been noted the authors I have adored for what they've reflected, and this simply continues that adoration. I show what I would like to continue of them. Despite the venerable likes of G.E.M. Anscombe, Hannah Arendt, Derek Parfit, Bernard Williams, and other commendable efforts, modern *moral* philosophy – whether formal or informal - seems neglected beyond, in methodical form, trying to judiciously reflect all the sides of an answer to medical issues and ethical action (abortion, euthanasia, etc.), and even outdated *duties*, and not so much an overview of - if not of ethical systems - the *meaning of morality and psychology* in a secular age, still holding modernist rejections and certitudes, that has been touched on yet still disfavoured for political expediencies, rebirthing and transplanting an ethics of old, and sceptical fashions. In short, it more often focuses more on avoiding basic conflicts of interest and legalism over defining and dissecting a good moralism.

The subject of real morality is still left, eventually, to the pious. And that does us an injury and disservice. When moral philosophy is most commonly considered it is either professionalised and academic - and so not public or influential - or when it is *public* it amounts to platitudes or derisive *self-help* none will (or should) take too seriously; or is, again, left to those haughty moralisers with an arrogance we would not wish to suffer under. Even worse, eugenics at the expense of the ill and disabled is still more popular than it should be.

Ethics, and then morality, carry on almost through sheer force of will, or ignorance, faith, or tied to social mores that we don't dare look into very deeply - reflexive livings even when one can found oneself on easy bases or in a religious author (though there is little wrong with that compared to categorical dogma). If all we really have, at the base of the universe sieved through all deduction, is faith in our stock... then countenancing that case is important, not passé, and we can still maintain standards and limits refuting those more pallid scepticisms, as well as fanaticisms. We can still have some measure of Reason while in Hell.

This type of *accounting*, not a systematising which we must not have, a modern scope upon the order of things, has afforded its contributed claim, a modest moralism, in the said efforts above - in the aforesaid praise of last-century figures *of responsibility.*

Those to see as shoulders to stand upon and live up to in good faith.

And yet this idea of contemporary morality, and wider ethics, in an absent or indifferent age unable to have unsatisfactory *returns* (how to preserve moral sense under nihilism while not loaning oneself to extremes or false *cures*) is becoming a boorish topic for me, in my fixation on it, in my dissatisfaction with all the hard-worked results and intricate attempts at the renewal of past things. It is still a shtick we can't overthrow. What I want, in a Camusian sense, is a "*modern tragedy*" for my reflection. One which can eventually denounce tragedy after its diagnosis and be undeluded by exaggerated visions of the past or future. Certain faiths cannot claim a monopoly on what we see, even loosely, as virtues; nor as the only type of restorative fiction and function capable for us to deal with our terror.

If I were to write (with more doting effort) on this most weighty of subjects far more thoroughly and with diligence, I would need something different from the usual fare of *formality*. I still attest to the worth of myself and the worth of outside things through external voices. This means I am far less original. I am less meditative, then, meaning less absorbed in my own confidence - lacking it – to come up with such things on my own. I have no War I lived through, no long age of experiences, but only my own mangled set of feelings and deathly compromise as I face a nearer doom than my peers and friends. If I do attempt *formal* work I would reproach the confines of scholastic *formality*; the professionalisation that suppresses thought more than any outside dogma or repression. Let alone making something unenjoyable or even impossible to read...

157

To write on this is to not write so plainly and miserably on events. Nor so rigidly. Nor in firm *reports*. Nor any defined set of directives or demands or decrees and dogmas and whatever other doctrines one could use to embolden and employ themselves. My home is not just some pile of professional bricks. It is my meagre being.

It still so wants you to make yourself alone, even if one must be resigned eventually to live with oneself, yet it has its hypocrisy and if you dare mention others you must detail every tiny aspect of bibliography. My thought was thought by another? We know this. Am I to care? I could follow that [that stringency], but I am not cut out for it. I crave vapidly, but also in a dearest sense… external feelings, themselves chaotic, disseminated to approve and colour my own mismanaged name of a soul. As much as my own unhealthy experience… my sourcing of others is not part of scholarly tradition.

To speak of morality is to speak of a messy identity, and where I may only be able - in a more adequate way - to speak of dreary self-feeling, and not write some grand tome on other peoples, I must, I think, without being prophetic or arrogant, speak of myself but with vital assurances. That is what I would write. I must name these assurances in a project I'll not be able to complete. Sifting through many names and ideas, lists and personalities, in the desperate quest for this reassurance... an outline of my own modern ethic may be surmised (if it must be corralled and narrowed-down for ease) in four parts: Aron. Camus. Unamuno. Weil.

Again, this is a dissemination, never a full appropriation. If I had the energy I would order a comprehensive treatise, of a sort of grandiloquent modern moral guidance (not a formal decree or screed, of course), founded mostly on the convictions and sentiments of these fine examples, and a study of their biographical and intellectual histories - well-situated.

Aron is selected for a particularly commendable rigour and thoroughness to historical overview: a modest search for basic truths or the elimination of lies, by a broad sociology; and a prescience in sight of events. I'm trying to indicate a certain namesake Aronian realism, if not *realpolitik* - the idea of what one should do within what they can do. And, too, a conduct and conscience in how to react effectively, not just emotionally or violently. Aron's *Memoirs* reflect such modest diligence and care.

In this sketch of a project Albert Camus and Simone Weil (with realistic reservations) attend to further details in conduct, behaviour, justice; and Unamuno - while not alone in this - helps reflect the stark, frightening prospect of founding an ethic in full knowledge of a lack of 'solid foundations', unable to so simply forget the dirty implications and worries of extreme scepticisms. Perhaps, in words used yet again, of nihilism; now very much saturated by over-definition.

This is the delicate, conflicting process of thoroughly rejecting the cold indifference that nihilism, or anomie, begets to the uninitiated while not forgetting its existence. Begrudging nihilists are still anti-nihilists. The term nihilism is equally throwaway as well as too precisely designated, but it vaguely expresses a sure truth - of doubt. And I cannot emotionally nor principally forget that no matter my effort. Want to stop doubt? Stop existing.

Other figures could perform this *task* and fill or replace the roles of those I've elected to represent particular behaviours - holding similar theses - but for brevity and by a studied preference I would attempt to illustrate the histories and circumstances of these figures, to situate them, and then extract their personalities to demonstrate something of my own ethic/aesthetic without being so anachronistic. A personal story attempting to poke at a higher profession. While belonging to the past century they are present enough to our atomic and technological malaises. Our issues. Current fashion and interests, etc.

None of these figures could be taken in-full to help explain my own convictions. I cannot embody them fully and it would be wrong to do so. The required godlessness, a blasphemy, of Camus outweighs the Christian sense of Weil or Unamuno - but the latter's encounter with the failure of strict rationalism to vindicate God, and then ethics, is important as a grounds for requisite epistemology and is associated with similar premises, incompatiblism, found elsewhere with myself and many of varied allegiances (Camus, Nietzsche, Kierkegaard, Lev Shestov, et al: not so alike in themselves but facing similar issues). And each figure provided in their own bordered way the significance of irreconcilability in concern for the choices we can make.

What is incongruous has power, and what is congruous is determined within the limits of subject boundaries, so where it can be grappled with (the thorough study of logics and empirical fact) it must be illuminated by a warning of incapability that does not exceed itself or usurp its own seat by over-insistence. This would be a substantive project in its possibility where, if brought to bear would be a detailed system of argumentation and theory aided, without shame, by past authorities.

*

Of who provided me the most of my literary inspiration, I have a long history of writing on Albert Camus. Camus is someone whom it is easy to be introduced to, with the colour of fame, but someone I actually cared to learn about extensively, and I daresay more accurately, rather than giving a banal and commonplace reading. I found such an assurance with Camus.

I discovered literature and philosophy during hospital admissions as a teenager.

I came across many obvious names and relatable works, and published my own reflections, but it was always Camus who offered me the most kinship and an aspirational image of what I could be were I less morbid, while, too, still retaining my ontological sensibilities. With me still trying to be reasonable as to not romanticise dead figures...

I read nearly everything - all that I could of him. His notebooks, private letters, essays, plays, novels... and I found such affinity in a totally decent, open-hearted man who could act as a rough image of the *moral responsibility* I wanted. I fear idealising him, and he knew fully well his personal missteps. I am sad at those who'll claim to *understand* someone after only reading one thing, as if the sordid life of a painter would be known entirely by one painting of a vista... He offered the only literature I could truly say I really loved. He showed an ethic and spirit, journalistic integrity, truth over expedience, standing against death. I don't care how facetious that could be, that so many could misuse, mislabel and misname him; I know there is much that is better in its quantity and its quality, but he seemed the least wrongheaded, at base, in what I would care to see. What was well-known and accessible was reasonable, much else was misunderstood, but once you'd care to get through it you could see it'd have the right tone. I once tried to dislike all his work and his life as some outside experiment and could only recoil at the terrible attitude it was to hate such things. And as such he stands correct at the closing.

For biographical coincidence, I too was a goalkeeper in my youth, and had to quit sports due to my ever-declining health. It was personal demands as well as literary (and philosophical) that created my image of a familiar aspiration, a familiar friend. An inspiration I could always return to. Camus, in his ideal form, represented an emotional place where I wanted to be, perhaps less adulterous, even if my reading was somehow wrong, but could never seem to reach considering the paranoia surrounding my hastening life.

A reiteration: beyond a diagnosis of the world as *Absurd*, his sensibility that is favoured is not necessarily for any typical *intellectual rigour* but for the right sort of comprehensive and measured sensitivity to his times. The right ethic in the face of cold things - a rejection of messianism, of Utopianism, or much else of anything, varied as those things are, that would want to justify the violation of man for abstract projects. That is not a pacifism, and indeed it does fight and revolt precisely against cruelties - it is a wish not to lower oneself to dogmatic extremes in the name of false or unjustifiable things. It is a revolt that says *no* to death and murder. This wasn't, obviously, some airy and clichéd thing. It looked cautiously at the lowliness of nihilistic possibility.

Camus held a scorn for pridefulness, a long history of pride and horizontal religions; a pride that is not the imitation of virtues, but a single encompassing vice of murder often held under the needs of *causes*. It is noting limits above that of wild possibilities - against those of disparate stripes who'd claim under the hijacked name of political *realism* to order the bloody sacrifice, surpassing borders of decency one should hold on to action, of the present for a future that does not exist. By the conservative mind or by the revolutionary… Even then, I would want to countermand claims of his time, that still live up to today, that while Camus can be respected for his distinctive and brave moral standing, his quality as a writer, commitment and responsibility (silent or not), and *the* feeling given in his works... there is the claim that his philosophising specifically and technically was *puerile*: in the words of Raymond Aron (Aron later gave more praise to the writing of Camus, the man himself, his journalism and wartime record, as well as agreeing, reasonably, with the sentiments of *L'Homme révolté* in his own *L'Opium des intellectuels*. But he pointed specifically and briefly to a regular criticism of the man in his [lack-of] technical - scholarly - ability with the requisites of drearily formal or academic philosophy. He simply wasn't too thorough and could contradict himself). Perhaps Camus is my heart and Aron is my head?

If you are to further the claim beyond disliking a lack in rigour, I think, again, it is more stylistic than anything else. And that it is not a true indictment of the finer components of his thought despite the less methodical nature of his words, its contradictions, compared to his contemporaries or to professors who still lack the moral punch or a good gist.

That while he himself would deny the label of a *philosopher*, and never wanted to be a philosophical genius, it is precisely the honesty and modest sentiment of Camus, that knows its subject and knows his limitations, his doubting self, that gives his own mild philosophy, his style and his politics, a strength over that which was extant to him - in his reaction to tyrannies. And what, with prescience, he said would likely come after him. A farsightedness and long-view that saw how easy it was to desecrate the present: by futurisms that would hold the need and disregard of violence for better tomorrows, or presents - skybound or earthly - and likely not of any reality. Aron would, in a banal sense, agree but by a more thorough, cooler sociological dimension that would give literary flair more credence.

The flat condemnation of some ability does not remove some truth, and designating the man as something else - better literary than philosophical - points at supposed contradictions (being *meaningful* while describing meaninglessness) that Camus astutely recognised anyway, and chose to live with regardless in order of a better living. *Lettres à un ami allemand* would easily and straightforwardly show this love of our insisted meaning within the obvious thought of a meaningless nothing... Need I cover this man with some extended biography? He fits my own description. He was weary. He could not give everything an explanation. He could not order all of the world under definitions, such as a *philosopher* would often attempt to - more than just asking questions. Again, to have philosophic thought without contradiction is to have thought that can only be facile. Even when one's thought is less studious and painstaking the actual point of the man was nobler - a truer response to anomie than death; or intricate theory and system that would lead to death anyway. One may not wish to follow his line of argumentation, or note ironies, yet it is difficult to come away from reading him and not have your vision remedied.

Hannah Arendt declared him "the best man in France." And was likely very right in doing so. He has more to praise and more to live by kindly, as a reluctant moralist, perhaps one of the best *moralistes* of his time or since, than those equally, creatively, but wrongly and irresponsibly *engaged* in his contemporary debates - or otherwise disposed to harmful readings and defiantly harmful practices.

His worries still mean much; if even more than what succeeded him. We still have *guillotines* to get rid of and we still have murder to contend with. Suicide is still as important as Camus' aphoristic opening in *Le Mythe de Sisyphe* suggested it was; even in its simplest form with any change in formal tendencies or the cultural landscape. I can only recommend more thorough readings of and on figures so easily misconstrued. Fame colours the perception we have of old, dead men and women... let alone those still living. Yet it doesn't take much reading to move beyond misunderstanding. And Camus isn't too hard. There are those given false definition to make it easier to bring them down... The *sentiment* was always more important than the pernickety stuff, in the end, as that is what had the result that mattered. What stood in the end? What use was *rigour* if it did not need to overcome an emotion? It certainly has its place and its need but that cannot come at the substitution of better conduct - where one is meticulous but for awful reasons. What use was exactitude if you could not overcome arrogance and murder? Such a call does not ask to throw all scholastic rules to the wind (which would be the easy and stupid inference), and to think that is what's being advocated would be insulting. Tony Judt would say that we need a basic chronological understanding of history and context before we set about interrogating the story. We need a basic order of data before thinking of the past under a narrow lens as a set of prejudices and lies, i.e. moralising history before understanding it. To avoid misunderstanding I want to make a brief distinction in that there are lazy historiographies that take a moralising stance before prudent understanding of time and place, and then there are people who believe they are doing correct and precise philosophical and historical work because they are conforming to particular rules or frameworks and established traditions - that have more of a political bent than one of historical honesty.

And these are replacements in easy form for intellectual responsibility. Moral and/or political judgements need to be made after you have set yourself into a place where your sentiment is not just the world rigorously described, but understood. What I mean by *sentiment* is that if you are to extract a moral story from a philosophical treatise or a study of history (or to be a moralist in the vein of someone like Camus, who was not the best academic), your predilection towards those ends cannot be either lazy moral interrogation or a love of academic formality and what is typical in such exacting standards, which are intelligent and well-written, but not intellectually honest and so, as is the case, a bad history. Plenty of artsy anarchistic sorts without rigour are equally annoying compared to those who care more about grammar than they do actions. No. It is merely a sight of better priorities and artistic merits.

As for Camus, in the last analysis… Camus was a star, and the forefront literary contribution to my life.

*

But of my own future… the title of this section. What I would write? What can I do? Could I do the above and have *a substantive project where, if brought to bear, would be a detailed system of argumentation and theory aided by past authorities?* Let us be as frank as possible. I would do this if it were not for my own brevity. I have to be candid with my ability. It is a misfortune that my personal necessities mean I am a frightful and frenetic mind, and my personality would void any serious or formal attempt at this. I am far too lazy as well. I can see and diagnose something irresolvable, and even actionable effort cannot overcome my end.

A careful, loathing, dithering consign of illness stammers you. I'm just too ill to write so full a treatise, and I fear that much of this writing is just a form of masturbation. My possible ability to get slightly better within the confines of my state is hard to reach by mental motivation too. I can't do as others do very easily. Maybe I stray too far into pre-Freudian complexes and fetishise my limitations? I am not sure how I could escape myself anyway. It must be stressed that I am simply unable - lacking mental and physical fortitude. I can recognise and scrutinise this blockade, but not without painlessness and I have to concede a prognosis. My ills, pathology, its restraint and extent, foil my possibilities in study or work but I cannot resign myself to nothing, then, before I perish. I have an odd lack of working responsibility which means a bemusing sort of freedom. But that freedom from conventional acts obviously has its own horrors. If I do not have the room to study so deeply then I will make room for art.

Unless some miracle amends what has always been maintained of my upcoming fate, then I can hint at what I had wanted, I can show a glimpse of greater things by association, and perhaps I can show some memorial to what I was for those dearest to me - as a final reprieve for my wearied self.

I will continue a project of love.

CORRESPONDENCE, LOVE

A previous assertion: there is a rejection of romanticism, in how it pressures one to forcibly engage in love at the pain of shame, but not, no matter what strictness could be admirable, a repudiation of a need I cannot do without. Bitterness is my only recourse in ignoring it, I cannot disown beauty, and my own self-entitlement engages me to love what love should be.

I recover this rare pulse with physical interactions, from being so alone, and it is only so moving because I lack tacit motive to be social in a great sense I would often desire, as I have always had an affinity, whether through the toil of illness or other shortcomings, with loneliness. When I see my previous words on this same subject - my history of sociability - I can see a former situation of indignant youth, maybe anachronistic, but it is not now alien to me. In absence of long-term lovers or confidants I reflected upon myself publicly - in publications - as a haphazard replacement. I created a novelty in the act of publishing to help myself and my esteem.

I have always thought I can scrutinise my social impotence well, my own representation of character, my own peculiarity and my own fault and reckoning. There is a history of self-isolation, but one easier to describe than explain. It still lingers that this is my own inefficiency, but I am not a flop or inept once set in interactions beyond boisterous crowds. I grow vulnerable there, but in other groups or singularly I am mostly eloquent. There is instead a struggle to prioritise correspondence, and its realisations in hindsight which I am sure are common to many. I've always granted a disconnected solipsism to my own interactions, as in with friends, that shows difficulty if I am attempting to fix things - for manifold reasons. I struggle to analyse the finer points of this without destroying my self-worth or being left empty.

I know there is a lot to me that causes this poor performance. Sometimes it is fright, lack of intuition, poor judgement or romantic desperation which creates my trouble with arranging interaction, or I can just as offhandedly hold responsibility to sociological events... and the alienations of modern communication and messaging. There is another source. Being unabashed with announcing my death, once inevitably asked... but that can wait.

It is not in the swing of interactions where I am incompetent, or feel dumb and inadequate. It is in the preparation of interaction, or in retrospection. Reciprocity as and when it happens is not a nervous affair. I orate well, I take conscious diligence to listen to those I care for, and I know I care genuinely. Daily ablutions and reflection mean I try to assuage the bitterness that comes from knowing imperfect people; I know with the complexes of pain that impetuousness, rudeness, and anger should not last long against what are minor slights, or affronts, so such breakups and forgetfulness I try conscientiously to treat with a needed forgiveness often mislaid in fits of annoyance and dejection; by many, as the estrangement from social feeling, this severance, greatly torments the heart and produces cruelty to all involved.

Wasted time and energy is not something that is contended simply. And we have shown here the weaselling attempts of someone seeing uses but lacking solid capacities. So what is being aimed for, within myself and with my conduct, when I see this failure on mine or others' part in social reciprocity?

This afar, noble attempt, so adrift and tantalising, is to make a more prudent use of this suffering and failure in these events without turning to ecclesiastical luggage or false virtue when we are trying to make sense of them. Suffering has an excellent possible use above a long, single note of rationalisation that tries to discipline, and then punish, and fool one into a lack of depths. That is to say, I want to try and have a better comprehension of social woe when it is extrapolated.

It [lacking bitterness and learning from misdeed] is an effort I see neglected and one I try to keep with a mature sense, a sort of Stoic's responsibility, but a slight is still hard to forget and I have always managed to vainly hold the idea that my pathological suffering put me in need of more support - and that was socially neglected.

I could accuse that as too indulgent, self-pitying, but I can only describe it more than I may definitely conclude or condemn. Others have surely and thankfully attested to my need to be cared for, if my self-worth cannot comfortably say so. Out of loops, the unclearness of reciprocity, antagonisms, things left unsaid; these are hard to conform with and I can offer only a mixed and faulty experience. The oblique, heavy hidden lives behind friends you thought you knew, left unsaid, while the course carries on nonetheless...

There is somehow a difficult time in the preparation of being able to do something, logistical organisation, multiplied by the lack of clarity or inadequacies regular in most communication that bothers me so dearly. Failed communications in your different correspondences can still, at least abstractly, be seen for what they are: where embarrassments or acceptable worries cause the breakdown of defined talking, of distinguishing what your correspondence is and what it means, so they can maybe be more satisfyingly accepted, endured, and less begrudged. We cannot afford Sartre's idea of social *transparency* in any practical hope, regardless.

The argumentation may not follow, but I begrudge more this ineptitude, an unfitness (mine and others), to the primary organisation of action, events, the prosaic organisation of social life and the simpler lack of repartee - over the lack of skill or finesse in the action of at least talking, through any means.

Maybe I am fooling myself? That communication recedes and slowly disappears between former friends is still my greater disquiet, not just failing to see people altogether, and I cannot truly cope with those failures? I can go long stretches without talking to others, and where there is the technology that means easy and instant communication (or the capability of it) there is still a problem of tone and clarity and how these technics delimit our motivations; how our surroundings differ our motivations, or a lack of sincerity as per digital anonymity. The digital world has a phantom mask that can be surpassed, but it is as much eagerly enforced as it is possible to overcome, remove, and use prudently. Perhaps, yet again, I am ruminating needlessly over my own failure to simply organise events? Whatever the case is, I just want more of a vital physicality that I lack so much.

I crave a touch I feel missing in my everyday distress - and I have always felt an absence of conscious care for my social well-being beyond familial and hospitalised attention, if not a lack of awareness for those who do care for me. As I know they do.

But my efforts are established as being restricted. I am unable, by my condition, to so easily further them. I always felt a lack of help, but did not feel free to be publicly upset for fear of accusation and causing upset, and could never not blame myself if I were explicit. I saw intimacy going astray, and the forgotten significance of friendship when abandoned to clichés and misplaced as a good topic for discussion, yet not analysed in some sterile way. Going out to do something, the scarce chance to discuss Orwell, minor pub visits, a holiday, seem far more serious to me when they are flippant things for others. I see friendship and become desperate. There is a physical conditioning of this desperation, though not anything Pavlovian. Illness conditions social view.

I craved, utmost, friendships to cry to and save me from what was so utterly and despondently tragic - that could never be retreated from in the truest way. An unspeakable melancholy. An immovable thorn. When I travel with friends I feel more alive than ever. I simply give-in to the common feelings I'd otherwise make distant. Much is said of what it means to travel, and maybe I could add to that later…

*

I am still oblique, and maybe I should taste my own words and give clearer examples…

I am as upfront with my condition as I can be, without being too morose, as I have to be. I accept comedy by my terms with it, as I cannot seamlessly live or love with people while lying about my many sufferings and hospital visits and treatments, and it would be impossible to lie about them as well as wrong to lie to them. This honesty is appreciated by some, if not immediately disquieting, but it has always meant an implicit obstacle with the possibility of love and romance. This may be my more earnest worry, over friendship, with whatever miniature differences there are.

Some stiff and snotty English gent deals with romantic passions, it seems old hat…

Yet there are surplus trappings. Once this is exposed there are few that may seem so willing to enjoy or accept this masochism. Descriptions of symptoms, the prognosis, things I will be explicit with, certain minds can forget them to live in moments or perchance accept a cold reality… but with no miracle cure in sight I am to be left as this expiring, chronic being.

I have been rejected after intimacies through fear, cowardice, worry and meek concern for harm. You speak of what you are and you could lose everybody. It is somehow, in a mixed and subtle way, speaking to me, like speaking to the recently bereaved; but rather with a slow persistence that won't leave unless you are dishonest, lying, or constantly deflective from what looms in you as you engage just in regular conversation. You are a reminder to happy couples, the blissful, to those with long dreams... that it would all crumple and crumble into naught.

To love that man, and the image he promotes? Would that be a form of self-harm? This accusing of oneself is not to crush others - as judge-penitents. It is not to confess my own sins and deprived body to condemn others. My solitude cannot be my pedestal where I flaunt and punish. I have to borrow reminders of positions to show that I am not being vindictive, nor so exclamatory, but saddened; descriptive of one's own malady as an honest and commiserative illustration.

Hardly any enterprise with such intense expectations could fail so regularly as love, in any case. But this case? This is a massive compounding of what is already a harsh trial. There's a greater sensitivity, time-bound pressure, the heightened temporal exigency, and more a want of honesty that others can say they are fine without. Maturity is still

not a force that could so easily overcome our

disappointment in failed love, and despite the

immensity of my pain I manage a dutiful, even forced

judiciousness and patience a lot of the time. Do I

have the currency for that? There's the trepidation

that I don't, and that I would do better to show people

their misgivings, their cavalier disregard, and help

them to grow in their integrity and wonderful

potential by revealing myself to not be

misunderstood; no matter how painful it would be to

them to be an example of shattering taboo. To give

them the light of death may be better than leaving

them adrift, some have said.

Do I care by showing the dire consequences of

people's bad actions or allow for the bliss of

clemency? I still don't know.

Transparent or not, I create a precedent for

the possibilities of future living, of prolonged love,

and I outline a cause for expedience in my want of lusts as well as more substantial affairs of the heart. I need to live and love quickly before time is spent.

Achieving worldly wisdom in humility and self-awareness still does not prepare for the final experience, for real grief, by plan and prediction. Virtuous instructions don't prepare one, coolly, in experience for agony. You cannot inoculate yourself, or tranquillise yourself, outside of words with a supreme effectiveness. You're too impotent and your mind isn't the psychic inquisitor of the heart. It's a poor old man giving occasional advice and direction. It may not be followed, and maybe sometimes it shouldn't. I won't say definitely and I lack the intelligence.

Circumstances give frame to the perceptions of thought at one or another time, and it is important to remember that strange while very obvious fluidity.

Of lost love: when another mistake occurs it opens a holistic lens, everything hits you at once, where the specific act of losing someone, whether it was clean and amicable or half-aware and stoned, is then seen as an integral part - of the sum of illness and condition. With the loss of distraction, again I am opened to seeing naked what I can cover-up normally by basic practices, as well as significant desperation. Of what being chronic, and soon enough terminal, means for anything I would do and be.

Looking through these lenses: being in terminal shoes provides some perverse satisfaction - in some possibilities - by setting the boundaries of the ground clearly. You can work to the deadline and explain your death in stern words for people to plan around. Being chronic, from one's birth disposed to differently look at things, there is a dim purgatory instead. We can try to trace the clouded lines between mental, chronic, and terminal phenomenology - we can note their intersections and their similarities, but here the description offered - both in view of love and life - is the almost rarer sort of long-worn, hard-learned, life-long suffering under progressive illness that has a neglected literature compared to the often suddenness of terminal scares or the erratic life of depressive mentalities. These are never distinct categories, but some measure needs defining for my ease.

With this lens, there's a rationalisation of feeling to try and cope with it, with the difficulty chronicity brings to love lost, but this comes at some expense where there is a struggle to give room just to feel what I am feeling without worry or shame. You fear your own bitterness, the reproach that is said is deserved from you, what another deserves in kind, by your own friends when caring for your view; and you beat yourself up over feeling passionate in your failure. So there's that which needs to pass each time... but when you live to love again, there is still the abject fear of your time being more precious than others, a coerced view of lost time, and the result is often a bleak self-seriousness covered with dry humour, a little frantically, and still weary in conscious dread.

I have always loved in my strained and worried way so many things about others, even those that went beyond what I'd ever understand. No matter what misgivings I'd have and compromises I could see being needed, I could not change much about those I loved without feeling guilty - and in wanting major changes to one's lovers one shows how they fail in loving, and harm those they adore. Nothing is enough for them and they must dream so highly. They become most adept at dreaming, of obligations, yet another each day, yearning for what they cannot discover and for fresh new demands. And then there's those who don't deserve love... I am left with a knowledge that love can't wait so long. A shared bedroom, a hand held in yours, I can't see much else that matters when very little matters much. It is not puerile or quaint to say it. It is just too commonly said in dull and repeated ways, emptily, without a real heart to it. What diktats and plans are so urgent and demanding? Do you need these patterns and strategies? I can't fulfil most, if any, and there's the sight of worse things that take priority: fear, a most awful of things. A fear of being alone before I go.

There is a layer that makes loving so much more desperate. The chronic sense is constant, ebbing, the flavour left in your mouth, only sometimes wrapped up and warped by everyday focus. You wake drunkenly at night, soft jazz humming as some atmospheric cliché, and see what is impending as you're wretched to its sight - by your lifelong condition. You know everybody will face it, but the saying loses its bite and has no true severity. It becomes meaningless to suggest to those full of life that they will soon meet an end. They will not feel it deep within their bones until too late. You have to stress again, once more, that for those *others*, those you fear hurting (as if one is egregious?) by saying you're special... their death is long away in their thoughts. We are all in the same boat, with death as the most certain of possibilities. But most cannot live, without exhaustion or paralysis, in constant fear of random leviathan attacks that will suddenly topple their boats. Their boats are intact and healthy. So they may sail to the many shores they can choose. The boat here is the similar, but it's already sinking. You were born with the water already lapping at your feet, and for what shores you can choose to embark to? Failure is more disastrous. What shore where there's a hand to hold can you get to when the water is at your neck and you barely have a boat left? Drowning is imminent. Maybe I can have this gloomy solipsism? Maybe I am allowed it after denying it so much, through fear or offence? After being assured that it is okay to say things and note these real phenomenological differences, can we have this? I am allowed my boat metaphor.

No one properly affords the cliché of urgency to life because vehicles could hit and kill you; they can live and ignore and be young and free and it is enviable. I am crudely poetic here, rather than attesting to psychological realities to substantiate the claim that death, illness and dying are not so often, frankly, confronted justly. I have done that before, I guess.

The Denial of Death[xxiii] will hold true, with the *heroic sense of immortality* still vibrant and gripping. Since birth my body was known to fall short, where most would have the far greater chance of prosperity and with little persistent alarm at disability. Many cannot conduct themselves on the '*what if*' of remotely possible accidents tomorrow, and less tormented are they by darkness visible. They do not ache so hauntingly and consistently in their everyday moves. They do not live by laboured breaths and can stand still most days without their bodies buckling, and they can run without dying in coughs and rasps. And when they do cough they do not feel the ripple of quakes and aftershocks course through their body as a forceful reminder of a protracted bodily reality.

They are not slowly dying by a chronic measure, they live with an attitude and manner of life unto life and not unto death, and their own pain is something else; by most reckoning a little less terrible, less persistent, and a little easier to endure by their happy distractions. It is not dismissive of them to say that. You hear it from them. They've said it to me as they offer false hope and plan things for 20 years time. They don't speak death's name and disbelieve the disabled's case. There are, too, the ubiquitous sorts that spit at wheelchairs and those with leprosy… They dismiss entire lives. Life itself, even.

There's those far worse than I. What of it? Seeing to those others far worse, there is no real help in the abstract measure of 'at least I'm not as bad as that'. You cannot minimise your pain by that unless you enjoy a vulgar sadism. Do not lie about your pain, Jake. The subsisting ill are still a minority. Afflictions for others can be brief, act towards the fact of death quickly, and not sustained so long, drawn out and annually. That offers no virtue but at least something phenomenologically different.

I'll be told of such energetic lives, be witness to them, and remain out of their reach. I cannot 'get action' [c.f Theodore Roosevelt][xxiv]. The myriad problems we all face in our degrees will be severe as one another, but different conditions mean different horizons and different ways of life. My own draws me hastily in to confront mortality, whether one was presupposed to existential query or not. When you know by so young that your life is destined to an early fate, it is much more pressing than the fortune's possibility of being in some chance accident sometime next week. You know you would go, you feel different, you live in another world, and you have less time for nonsense. But difference and the closing distance also enables you to ask questions - about yourself and also about others. To live exhaustively on abstract death, not just on definitive death…

"To gather ye rose buds is usually, despite film trope, a bravery out of range; off the array."

Infirm and ill; you may still not face the bare truth, you may conclude in naïve beliefs… but with me, I think warily and conscious of being haughty, I am *forced to nausea* and feeling - unable to trick myself and so simply dispel it. Morbidity imposes itself as a watchful guardian. On my shoulder my companion sits unresting. To not see death as an intrinsic part and not act with it, despite its obviousness, is not just an ignorance of everyday occurrence. It is not keeping in the front of one's mind... the dirty facts of war: what not seeing death produces in thought and action. It shows an obliviousness that justifies what would falter if it saw the truth of Oblivion. It extols in high concepts over what is small and real, and cheapens life itself.

"To answer your own question: Why did all of this happen to me? You gaze at everything with a parting and slightly sorrowful look... Almost from the other side... No longer any need to deceive anyone or yourself. It's already clear to you that without the thought of death it is impossible to make out anything in a human being. Its mystery hangs over everything. War is an all too intimate experience. And as boundless as human life…" – Svetlana Alexievich, *The Unwomanly Face of War*.

Most culture will not ever realise beyond the ephemeral sight of an occurrence… a sort-of Heideggerean living, every day, under the purview of death and threatening, life-shortening illness. Ideology will always favour a tomorrow, politic will always look forward to what is out of sight. It will not see a *long run*… Where you're dead. Montaigne wished to dissipate death by facing it head-on. This meant keeping it *in mind*. A trying task really… A most noble effort. What a sure and gentle guidance that man gave on facing death.

A majority will still always be able to pay to live as if they would not die, making use of their present time, no matter what death surrounds them even in the undertaker's office or the nurse's station. It is the guy next to you in the trench that dies. Not you. It couldn't be you... (That is certainly no condemnation upon nurses; who I owe my life to. Those doing hard and necessary work - and it would be imprudent to suggest that death is entirely a forgotten quantity when enough people would perhaps live more nobly in the light of death than I can most often see. But the tangled psychology of death and its mental distancing, the usual fare of how we live and forget, are still things to be seen).

Purchasing and unceasingly experiencing one's life with a view of mortality, especially one's own mortality, without the daily interruptions of the living business and activity is, at least roughly, made more possible (and even then slimly) through a direct self-experience of tangibly feeling weak, dying, delicate, debased and shortened in your own breaths; or a closeness to these things through work that reminds you daily. That does not mean the ill are virtuous by that case and are revealed to truth, but confrontations with bodily facts and conclusions on the use or uselessness of actions can be made, sometimes, more easily. In the right - or wrongly. You are closer by obvious facts to the realities of death and its implications - and pressured more than others to see it and think. Does that need to be said so convolutedly?

Do you want to force death? The premise? Slam your fist onto the desk and shout at them to look at it? You want to force that humility. Even if the patient is left only in conflict, stuck on the fault, remaining disorganised would be better than living so surely while *not dying and living forever*. It is hard to press home those facts even with demonstration. Inner turmoil becomes incommunicable apart from those fleeting moments when understanding could be clearer with pressing circumstances. And often, exposing to the ignorant their own offensiveness in not seeing the ill - either humiliating them or kindly awakening the realisation - can be upsetting not just to them but to you too.

It is hard to be in the best mood and say things politely on illness all the time, to always be well-behaved in pain, and live comfortably for others' sake.

There was a time when I was at university. I was alone in my room, reading or likely doing nothing. Tired as usual, unable to take out and order my medications so it would be easier to administer them and my treatments later. Independence is difficult when one is healthy. When unhealthy... Well, it becomes obvious... I was sat alone and wanted to move. Fatigue and lethargy always takes over and time would be spent asleep, not doing anything, spiralling down as I failed to care for myself. So I forced myself out to walk. I needed supplies and something to drink, so collected myself and went out. At first walking is fine, then one forgets oneself and walks too far. I would struggle walking back home. I over-estimated myself, desperately trying to exercise and be healthier to no avail, but did not want to go home empty-handed. Nor could I retrieve a proper shopping inventory. I wouldn't be able to carry anything beyond a small bag with some snacks as it would be far too heavy for me otherwise - while fine for most others. Even then my extra-light bag felt too heavy, and upon exiting Sainsbury's my body suffers. I cannot often acclimate to temperature changes without violently coughing, shaking, and then feeling stiff. I was already disheartened and gruelling enough, and then some member of the public decided to comment.

If one isn't abjectly crippled many will not consider someone as disabled or suffering, or in need of help, services, or facilities. Or just care.

Sometimes comments are offhand, or said jovially. I thankfully haven't suffered the most disgusting of offences where the ill are not believed or belittled and publicly emasculated by those with no understanding.

But this nasally, shrill, and baffled old woman decided to poke, with a biting tone, at the fact that I was coughing horribly, and in some pain, rather than offer help or aid. Why? Why take time out of her day to say anything, rather than just go home and rest? Why were people so preoccupied? Why this happy sadism? Normally, I would just humiliate the person bluntly. "No. I have a disease and will be dead very soon." Most do not comment further after that. This would go against my thought to not *flaunt* myself and my case, and I live with these regrets. But with this person, I had a weight upon me and I decided to destroy them. Not only did I declare my death, I declared hers.

I wished for it. I called her every name under the sun as this "bloodless cunt", with zero understanding, somehow deserved Hell for being so utterly stupid, inane, and crude in her remarks. In that moment she represented the whole score of people who knew nothing of psychology, or death, or of the entire gross human condition. Such comments show one ignoring things for their whole life. I felt awful after that. I did not need to insult this stranger so gravely. Teary and further disheartened, I left her blank and upset and commenced the long, long walk home. I couldn't call anyone to come and fetch me, and I would have to very literally drag my ailing body back to my bed. I fell straight asleep. Who benefitted from any of that affair?

There is still the case of one being anaesthetised to events by their regular proximity. By the metronome tick. Wretchedness and infirmities will be armoured against when seen so frequently, to facilitate our basic functions and process - to live more easily. Disorder, panic, and trauma are the more common happenings when *esprit de corps* and your unconscious guard are worn down by the violence of shitting yourself, lungs collapsing, and forgetting your parents exist or childhood memories every day. I want to believe that it is possible for most to see the defining cessation that is death, because I want at least a slim positivity from seeing that. I want care, from that. From nearly any faith, culture, class or upbringing, it is possible to encounter the dying and learn what it is to die by the only *view* we can have. We are mortal; that may be, and the heaven posed by those offering grand absolution, *the fix*, is yet again empty. There could be some next life, but such little comfort that is when facing the lime-pit, the executioner's pistol... And I cannot bother with it anyway. If I try to, I only feel that I am deceiving myself to feed a false dream. If our lot is complete annihilation then let us live justly; and not have our impending Oblivion seem as if it were justice. Death and illness and what these represent can be seen. Surely they can be learned from? Surely we can show love to what dies? An intuitive understanding of infirmity and deprecation comes from being ill - is possible from there - from unrecoverable illness, in a way more immediately apparent than if one can live more freely and healthily. There is a gulf between cultures: The Dying and the Immortal. Death is a thing, the most definite thing. It is unaffordable as anything else except by the most risky and fraudulent of leaps.

"The remedy the vulgar use is to not think on it; but from what brutish stupidity can they derive so gross a blindness?" - Michel de Montaigne

No matter the basal truths; the unconscious pervasiveness of immortality, by whatever biology and psychological condition, will hold forever such a sway that humility will always be more difficult than hubris. It is a vile world, and one can forget. I see a need to face it, for myself, instead. Now I need to find my solace within that.

My body and mind are aged before their time. I react instinctively to youth and have the response of a jaded old man; it is trying and an unfortunate removal of my patience. I stare blankly, but the remorse isn't defined, nor refined. There is good that will be failed, unsaid devotion, and finally after all the talk a sure emptiness. My time is more costly, and I feel that with a gripping severity. But to act? Improbable. That means one needs enthusiasm. To not be a sloth. To remove this, fire it, destroy it; no. It is a special fear, in its wake, a unique way of being scared; I don't have the currency to live unfearing and my terror is an exceptional terror above the extending others that walk straightly in the street. Am I too derisive? I really, really do fear that. The fury of realisation wears you out, a savage reminding, draining your colour and making you a pallid thing. The phenomenology of illness sets a tone, the sordid detail becomes too bare and, again, a clinging morbidity stays with you. There is something similar to what anyone would have, but compounded, enforced, and given a new sheen. Being brave does not give a true reprieve, you are not let free, and the death is not resolutely assuaged in its horror by any easy measure from being, either, stern or otherwise scared. But it must be seen. And through that… an isolated gnaw of impending doom, others can still carry on long and unremembering. You feel deeply selfish, alone, but there's little you can do to amend the position you're placed in, gifted an inquisitorial gaze; even with styled words a permanent vacation from grave thoughts is inaccessible.

They have work to be done, I guess…

*

So that is a case. And, in part, what love is in that case. How on earth am I to get over this? Should I? I clinically note the boundaries of romanticism, I clinically note my health, but I cannot crush my inklings through a process of equal pain and forgetfulness. I cannot be dishonest. I may not be alone, but I will primally feel alone and unconnected; neither helped to impossibly *overcome* by others, or by philosophy, beyond the appealing concord of propaganda from those totally decent, open-minded and open-hearted beings that I can order some affinity with. Affinity, but not a full reconciliation of grief, is all I can want to maintain. Philosophy won't reason-out our anguish, but an exposé may reveal something atavistic - an instinctual sympathy that may grant me a small measure of contentedness.

I am given the ability to expound on grief by my different proximity. I cannot afford an ignorance in some form of bliss from what is upsetting. This moroseness has formed me, I can see that, and I can choose to weakly hide it or show its true colour. I still don't want to have a dark literature. I need what is redemptive, but not what is a lie.

Looking at this writing in a disassociated way, it can reflect something I can see sometimes as admirable, and is most admirable when I can see what is written as sage advice from another. But there is always the difference between recognition and actually being capable of the endeavour to do something. When I see others having to deal with upcoming deaths I am oddly dumbstruck, as I think that saying something for its own sake is empty at best and insulting at worse. Funeral platitudes tire me. They even offend me. Those ceremonies, so acted and choreographed, the insular superficiality of rituals… they seem to terrify us more than the facts of demise itself, or otherwise exacerbate mourned pains by persuading the unthinking into making a spectacle of something for a day, then only to return to their daily apathy thereafter. The very notion of one's *deathbed*, surrounded by deathly dressed figures in deathly silence, not even speaking of the word 'death' as if they'd utter the name of the Devil himself? One may as well be dead already.

They set artefacts about to fawn over and weep, they act upon death as if attending a rare function, nor would they really give the arational detail of death its full face as they turn to platitudes. Deaths are more palatable when we are deprived of having to prepare grand ceremonies. A brusque statement, but I don't have many good funeral experiences…

For most ceremonies that is. Few can create good celebrations, but others, most others, engender restricted reflections made more morose than they should be. We aren't all in New Orleans. And ultimately, the agony is not contended. It is let out in one's brief spectacle - and the *everyday* still continues. The strangeness of death is not disarmed. There is, so lacking, a familiarity, amidst one's jolly steps and road journeys, death is not a frequent thought. When it is so frequent for some, it is paralysing rather than liberating. Few are truly worth listening to on the immense question. The diarist Barbellion is one of the best. The task or effort I would have in mind is to try and have the fact of dissolution as a liberating thing - while not being possessed by it, or creating a fetish. Death's clothing as a fancy dress doesn't help me.

There's a temperament needed, eventually. Where to stop and figure inescapable death means to give what *is*... its vitality. For enough of us, nothing was faced in the end. To live, to learn to live, to *philosophise* as if to learn to die... how rare a thing that is.

When I see others dealing with their own questions, I can offer something but my words could be empty no matter my intention or my severity. But I touch on something unhappy, no happy death, and again I get, as I am told, to set a tone. I would always see as selfish this idea of what I am faced with, that I was undeserving of love, and I ruined my self-esteem. Yet if I am able to make the pain of some others less terrible by my own example, then I feel I should give a hand to those I care for. I'm not for public duty, but I want a voice that can't be seen to be so vain. If I cannot do anything else, I want to care for those dear to me. And so I leave them my sentiments.

I could still never not fault myself for all my woe despite outside assurances… and I had to be told, remove my hate for myself, and be made to listen… that even though you are in a desperate situation, even though you would need more love and care than most, that does not mean people get to trample your precious heart outstretched and beating in your hand.

THE END OF CHRONICITY

As I continue to grapple with when my demise will
be, and the uneasy course of those last few years' up-
for-grabs, it is natural that I grow a little more
depressive no matter what lofty set of approximate
ideals I invoke to live.

I see the standard of the ideal Stoic which
we seem to want to preach. I'm rather dubious about
it. There is no whole rejection, but I want a
temperament of it. This is an undercurrent analogous
to the downward trend of my bodily health: receding,
gruelling, with fluctuations but the inevitable decline
that sees no upcoming repair. With what impression I
can give of myself and my feeling, it is a conflict that
is not exclusive between principle and natural

emotion that governs me. These terms, again, are not mutually exclusive and will intersect, rather obviously, but the principles I aspire to are these affirmations. They are loving affirmations in the face of a darkness. They are held in the adored words of others who too I admire as people, their lives, and possibilities still available regardless of fate. They mix with a guttural sadness, tragicomedy, an upset at the world but more an awful distress at myself and my perceived inability.

Every day I wake having to wash myself from a deep melancholy that flows beneath any easy talk. If I don't have that, there are days where I am just numb. It were as if I were a gormless animal who doesn't know where he is; or I could stare, as a cat may, at a wall for aimless hours - thinking of nothing (though it would be nice to think a cat would be musing happily).

Under all my effect, there is a child that shrieks and doesn't want any of this evil, any painfulness, the dread of being dead, and I would soon, and with a worrying haste, end it all. Treatments are painful. Stop that. Medicating. Stop that. Exercises and long car journeys. Etc etc etc... Please stop.

The process of thinking upon this becomes a tragic, then comic thing; and I must confusedly mitigate what is so dire and dreadful within me. Whether that be through some form of humour (one that makes some light of our absurdity - á la Beckett), or - if not that - then an unabashed frankness. I'm concerned that I'm far too depressive, and that the view from the likes of a Groucho Marx or a John Cleese, or *Beyond the Fringe*, etc - making light of the thought that nobody knows what they're doing or what's going on here - would be better than the similar themes coming morosely and more frighteningly from a Franz Kafka. But I'm afraid I lack that capacity for wit. I guess I like to be funny, but I don't think I can be *that* funny. To countenance this particular weariness every day seems foreign to those I'd describe it to, and is the hardest feeling to convey.

I regularly have to go through courses of IV antibiotics, other medications, the details become less important... The regularity of these procedures hurt me greatly, as it acts as a slow reminder of what currently afflicts me and what will come. Heavier interventions, surgeries, great risks, utter failure, these are all calculated in both icy and in sentimental ways. Parental wishes, doctoral demands, they are all weighed and judged in the kaleidoscopic mess of conflicting reasons and emotions.

I am not here to pander to those medical and medicative specifics, rightly or wrongly, as I would not want to bore with formal details of hospital notes.

I have said this already. The hardest thing to convey in my understanding is what I am faced with at a prospect of *getting better*, when I am shown the outside successes of others, and a chance of a slimly healthier living as well as the certain chance of an end - in the mind of the long and perpetually ill. This is always abstracted. The complexes of another are seen as if they could fit seamlessly upon your own delicate situation, where force of motivation and action will surely help and straighten-out the whole mess.

A whole life of experiences goes into developing what one is; and the thought of histories abstracted, people abstracted, ideas taken as tokens applicable to anything with enough finesse or brute force... I have never been able to accept this. We have equal parts anachronism, more obtuse solipsism, a taking of one's own boundaries as those of the world and anyone else; to flatly reject those possibilities seems scary? To be frightened and terrified at returning to a possible normalcy you never had: how could they not see that? There is a faintest chance of a new life you cannot exaggerate or invest hope in.

So much optimistic power is put into the hope of fascinating technologies and new developments. For some it seems easier to invest in them, within or without illness. But again we must note the differences of personal and ill phenomenologies; and the difficulty of experiences. To bring yourself up so high in that hope only to crash in inevitable failures you've been preparing for in many years' making, with so many peers already gone; it needs to be seen how such long experiences wear and bore on you.

It is denied, by passionate wishes, that faced with bright new circumstances one couldn't react with ease, by protocol, and that my entire mismanaged mess of thought and experience would mean I am set to fail - fulfilling my own prophecy or not. That failure could be recognised but not mended. It is the faulty path of convincing another of a different phenomenological horizon.

No matter if events could somehow, by their miracle, refute me… someone will have this anchor. Death still comes, and new transhuman developments are pitiable, as of yet. And even with their becoming there is the elementary philosophical mess. The drive to make it all better is so desperate that it can lead to nightmare denouements.

Stressed out, everyday shit, it is hard to foster solidarity of feeling for more than a passing moment or day. Demands will supersede immodest and impractical terrors. My grief is not so animated and active always, but numbing and immobilising. This doesn't reflect a usual picture of what despair is considered to be. It is the *wrong* mode of grief… as we seem to have more sympathy for outbursts and shock than what creeps on you slowly and looms; with desperate whispers and crooked steps.

One is expected to be contented and positive, yet seeing a real lasting happiness would always arouse the suspicion of something wrong, and melancholy will still face gross reproach. And that's in any case... In seeing what is saddening culture is disgusting. It is insulting. It lacks a true sight or consistent awareness of frailty. I cannot begin to fathom the chemical mix of interventions for my health, my whole life; and the resultant psychology provoked from that, and from a differed phenomenal view, sorely and gravely institutes a mind. I may not have some ratomorphic behaviourism, but there should be note of life's ambiguous and stricter influences.

"All of what I do in *Philosophy* is bundled with the refuse of illness."[xxv]

There's damage done, and I have to find another course of endurance.

My *philosophy* had to be an alleviation of immediate and prolonged pain, to allow me just to live - let alone subsist. It was not a curiosity first found in any derivative Aristotelean 'wonder', so inert, which eventually sucks you in to its own steel trap. Thinking you may out-think things. Epistemology-*proper*; alone? No. I had to see traps at the first step. And actually help myself.

How to make use of physical pain, more so, prolonged and illest disease: when the whole heart, mind, spirit... these are synonymously used terms and I austerely side with a boring account for what a person's essential element is... when one's whole emotion turns inwards and petrifies, if it cannot openly weep, there is an understated awfulness. Poetry attempts to reflect the substance of this, to communicate the idea, but it often falters at expressing the calamity. Does poetry really paint the war well? It is rare for it to do so well. You could reject wholly the limits of everything, embrace what is outside any real sight... a type of intellective suicide that is beyond my reach. Or you could more prudently accept, with a starkness, the tragicomedy. Naked to the unknown. Facing it. Always facing it. There's a baffled indecisiveness to face. It is a most humbling reverie that my burdensome tones could not merely be annoyances; that I could give a touching assurance and fraternity by saying something, and not hiding my woes. I have comrades under siege, by the same malady; I can give them the friendship of a shared experience. The sublime service of a language of the dying... to squeeze the hand of these intimate peers so bereft of their warmth. To have a dialogue into the ether that may be received.

I spoke earlier of being unable to build oneself with just oneself. It was more obvious why when you felt alone and that was crippling. When you feared the bitterness of solitude, and how painful and frightening that would be. To have an amicable capacity, and to have oneself evolve in decency, most would need the Hell of others. To extol in pure solitude is unavailable to me. Sometimes it is enviable when one can do it. A point needs to be made and repeated as it still doesn't gain purchase. Cases of individual pain being *worse* or *better* than one's own or my own do not help us by comparing them in some quantitative measure of what is more important. That is why I feel inconsiderate, and reticent, in managing to say I am different compared to most, that I am rarer; as their own suffering, by my confession, would seem meagre and devalued - they think. To say all other sufferings under the most abject are not worth concern by that reference is a destitute lie, a subterfuge and deflection, it does not make one's own slaughter any easier that it comes later.

Because rural children in distant lands die horribly doesn't mean one's worries are worthless, nor do those atrocities miser suffering. Instead, what I can do is foster a natural liking and comprehending of something - and a guidance I cannot myself easily perform. In suffering we cannot afford to be so competitive.

*

Here's the snag - so disassociated from my peers: prolonging my life starts to become, soon enough, an act of 'prolonging for the sake of prolonging'.

It is not a healthy maintenance where I may be productive and more importantly be *happy* (let us not take this word so lightly and conventionally) or accepting. It is a long, slow, suffering crawl that is sour, instead of short but sweet. If not sweet - I sadly must doubt that - then lessened in gross pain. I am having to measure that as well as facing a death that reduces me to indecision. There's a moderate ground to find that is obscured and clouded, as ambivalence to life weighs against the want of affirmation. Suffering is weighed alongside subsisting, and to persuade others of these differing weights means moving through impassioned desires. When I face a premature end, not just the generality of pain, I can only hold this repetition as I bluntly try to stay straight with my drenched order of thoughts as well as my daily motions. In this untidy bag comes a taut balancing. Austerity with unfetteredness, acceptance with revolt, sceptical one day and the next day an Epicurean - in vague terms.

This is a continued use of high concepts ham-fistedly describing basic understandings, and here it does a sad job in defining things improperly, unreasonably, rejecting and affirming itself equally. I value the want and wisdom of others immensely, who could with an enviable strength... marvel at life and want to live enduringly. And if I could, I would just follow those words. They have words above what I could say. I've said them to myself and understood them from those I admire, but I am still my own problem. Seeing something sage is fine in recognition, but I'm still emotional, worn, and tired. I'll write down an ideal, this is out of my control. Ideals are bigger than I am. I have, too, a history of descriptions against life, almost avowing a different sort of early death; but I at least murkily stressed their merit as descriptions of passing thought that I saw as important to confront. To reject or affirm, again I am always torn.

I can agree with a distaste for the shadowy pseudo-intellectualisation of and by the artistic, but I sit in the artist's seat. To serve, to do just, the fright of the *Pensées*[xxvi]: I want to be quiet - slow - in the way of being temperate in my inner conduct. With trying a little tenderness. There is little rush I can have for plans no matter my expedient body. I have to become less tense and agree a defiance while knowing my place. It is a capitulation to inability, though not resigned to life and ideas, served with awareness and love.

We return to the beginning of this work... the *Struggle*... I show that I want something fundamental from what is base, what is palpable, what I may taste and squeeze, because I cannot find anything fundamental elsewhere. If I accept a void it is metaphysical, in dismissing notions, not human. I had to remain sentimental eventually after my own coldness. These replayed feelings of placement and tangible sensations hold for me something dear with the vacancy of the spiritual world. There is the tie to this harsh idea of life's general character (what is amoral is still cruel to human emotion); and my self-seriousness, soppy and stern, draws on the repeated point held paradoxically.

Escapism in grandiose terms I find hard to agree with. There is escape in both the vertical aims of faith and the horizontal aims of the secular religions as their own nightmares. One leaves no room for dreams, but daily one keeps taunt and revising, as their vital thread, treading the narrow path of a truthful solidarity. To honesty in all our limits, primarily, before we go about touching wildest fantasies and visions. I can agree to a mild, tamer leisure as a fairer thing. I want to offer solace as I feel so much sorrow, but get stuck in my own worrywart misery. I still want passion with this leisure. It is not overly complacent, it has the fury of lost time; maybe it is *pagan*, meaning heretical? *Greek*. Maybe it would have been nice to be initiated at Delphi?

Dionysius speaks necessarily. So does Sisyphus. Remember to scorn Icarus.

A most basal idea of physicality has importance for a muted reason... What we cannot see will still be so terrifying. Creations to pretend we don't die won't help me, though nor would false hope in hotel rooms. What is physical does not distinguish merely some pale diversion, Hume's backgammon hedonism, for there needs to be held, too, an accord and condolence with what we direly see and cannot see. The apprehending of what we are confounded by has to be soothed by acknowledgment of the unanswerable, but we should not corrupt our resultant playtime into something that makes us hungry and cold. Into tactless hedonism. A sensualism that is unlimited and utterly naked becomes weak and obtuse. My struggle to hold the physical as a tantamount, paramount thing is stifled by what I've already said in its misuses; but all maxims will be misheard and misused by some crowd, and we cannot allow them to steal what is dear.

Meaning becomes a skewer to these misusers and misers who divest and kill us. We can comprehend something else to give us flavour rather than models and schemes.

In its replacement of a cosmology of escape my basic physicality cannot become as brutal and likewise - urging horizontally to cruel ends instead of vertically - in a wrongheaded retention of the same hubris. Humanisms of progress amount to the same flaws of spirit when without a quiet tempering, a mediation, and sensualism is still our vital aspect, if, *neither weak nor obtuse.*

Once more I must value love, friendship and knowing humour so seriously. These so common of ideals are given such a facile, paltry, scant and ineffectual treatment by so many common publications. The offence these outlets cause is

236

exacerbated if we see that they are taking vital and, dramatically, essential aspects of life only to (again) miser them and turn them into tat to be sold - appealing to our lowest instincts. They should do better to help themselves, and perhaps their so many readers.

Being alone is tough, and strong beyond any usual spirit when it is rarely comprehended with or exalted in without bitter pride. I am not strong, most are not. We have to be there for each other... together in our individual loneliness. Cliché should be seen through and suffering does not become a virtue that solves itself. It doesn't do that. If you keep what is yourself, and are not tranquillised by it, then it will stay. It is a question of coping, not of elimination - what is ill returns and remains.

Dying young is maybe different from dying old, where one could finally be *glad* to end a long toil... I am still wary of blunt stoicism. It seems as if

237

it is a sort of subterfuge. A trick. It seems, even, in its cases of public house stupor where ragged men proclaim they should be shot before dementia, as if it would be plain ignorance; and the wish to be shot before hardships is rarely fulfilled. And so many would die... naïve? I would be fooled to think elimination of emotion, or the hijacking of positive emotion, was possible and that I could cure the pestilence. I cannot forget wholly, but am allowed to for some time; to function. I cannot make wallowing in the swamp a virtue, and there is some contentment we'd surely deserve. It is too hard to be so dreary. I can't be a masochist.

I have escapes, but they can never be absolutes. I have unfortunate sights forced upon me, but I cannot be atrophied or left to the wild. It is specious and muddleheaded rationales that suggest we can truly escape the unhappiness and foreboding; that, somehow, what is terrible is easy to endure...

To not fear what we cannot feel? We fear precisely that we have no more sense, no more thought, the waste of efforts that cannot be replayed with no eternities to stray into.

To not love, link, nor think; to be annihilated against an essential eeking for sustenance. There's the animal fear the dissonant mind could, *could*, weasel itself out of. The body less so. It takes a unique constitution, armoured against its own essence, to find a peace that is not taut and unsure. Or it takes some long-worn and aged wretchedness. Fear cannot be escaped if one wishes to remain alive. Most talk of peace is stasis, and a lie.

To out-reason this heft is to ossify.

*

I kept something Kantian with me, beside my weary reservations, some duty; I cannot aspire to the hero -

making a virtue of misery (I have never intended to make my descriptions, knowing death, *virtuous*) - I have never had a place for sainthood either, making virtue miserable. I can only suggest a wisdom in our description of things.

Transcendence does not mean to find mystified elevation; nor am I to be annulled to the atrophied sensibility of the ardent rationalist. I never learned to accept myself, and my narrowed vision, and I really simply should have. Too much was beyond me and my understanding, all I should have done was accept.

The *trembling* philosopher, as Voltaire puts it, is desperate to know the world almost fully. So they, the great framers of definitions, if they're archetypal sorts of philosopher, attempt to systematically and as a wholesale ordeal understand the world as if it had a discernible formulation for all of its attending parts. When we are simply too feeble for that. We can touch on things, be thorough taxonomists in some case or so, but it is a matter of aesthetic that says the world is wholly cogent in our possible perceptions or that the world is externally made true.

Others can forget these comprehensive projects employed to comprehend things and live, some tremble in their subject, and some are naïve enough to think they can know it all.

In our areas we can examine, in language, in conscience, what are we to do eventually but give ourselves some levity, and, even, give up in *knowing it all*, give up reconciliation, or ideal, for our own good and prosperity? There are still enough injunctions and pretexts to say *no* against while recognising the failure of zealous ambitions. It is perhaps a wise move, of a better temper, to not feel bad for what is beyond you. But it is still difficult. Pride and relief are still possible while reconciling the world is not. Summer exists within you without removing the death from winter, and maintained is the fragile blossom on the spindly tree. The recurring words in these constraints of vision are not optimistic recipes. We have little use for those recipes in the extremes of our distress. They are, want is longed for, words of wisdom and of rarer courage - not absconding the world or oneself. A vulnerable meaning, frail but defiant, comes from knowing it all stops. It is not a sad philosophy one has if they dislike comfortable optimism. The sun and beauty are still there. What one has: it is sensitive to the world. *Concerned*, if grave.

It is not soft and merry with escape, nor hardened in armouring itself against cruelty by cold rationale. It finds a peace that isn't stasis, which is tautly balanced, equivocal, conflicted and unsettled. We touch on extremities both at once. With so many contradictions I would hold, there is an equal

opportunity. A joy that is so splendid, and a most
cruel, severe of pains. Absolutism, of this or of that,
so *sure* of the escapes, is mistaken as a taste for the
truth. And I remain in the end a fumbling boy.

So, physically, with an openness of heart,
we may hold each other in sympathy of what will be.
Without these confidences life becomes an
exhausting unhappiness. Gratitude alone can suffice
for us to live. We push the stone together, calmly,
while seeing when our time is up - at rest. We may
grow less afraid in each other's arms, mildly putting
aside the grim things for a short while before they
come. We two dead things may live...

I tremble at what's here, so soon, pointed; haunting
and corroding me. When I do, I will die wearing two
faces.

[i] CFTR – Cystic Fibrosis Transmembrane Conductance Regulator

[ii] To the knowledge of his doctors, Jake's CFTR mutations are totally unique in combination, and have never been documented together at once before in another patient.

[iii] Arthur Rimbaud (1854 – 1891), French poet, a known libertine and restless soul who travelled extensively after ending his literary career at the age of 21.

[iv] Before I went to university my parents had high hopes for the prospect of me being less educationally regimented and more able to expand my learning horizons, as I seemed to be limited within secondary education. Unfortunately university was not for me, considering my health as well as the narrow nature of my university course, and while my parents were at first enthusiastic for me to continue my studies, I was unable to. Eventually we all understood and I left university.

[v] Dr. Bernard Rieux is the narrator and main character of Albert Camus' *La Peste (The Plague)*. A practical man, Rieux struggles ceaselessly against the plague in the city of Oran despite his fatigue, his unbelief, and signs that his efforts are having little effect.

[vi] Heraclitus of Ephesus (535 – 475 BCE), pre-Socratic Greek philosopher, noted as 'the weeping philosopher', sometimes contrasted with Democritus (460 – 370 BCE), known as 'the laughing philosopher'.

[vii] Peter Wessel Zapffe (1899 – 1990), Norwegian metaphysician and mountaineer, noted for his philosophically pessimistic and fatalistic view of human existence, inspired by Arthur Schopenhauer (1788 – 1860). Zappfe's most significant essay, *The Last Messiah (Den sidste Messias)*, was published in 1933.

[viii] In Greek mythology, Silenus was a companion and tutor to the wine god Dionysus. The Phrygian King Midas was eager to learn from Silenus, and so captured him. When the king asked for his wisdom, Silenus laughed at him and shared his pessimistic philosophy that said it would be better for man to have not been born.

[ix] Further reading - *Amusing Ourselves to Death: Public Discourse in the Age of Show Business* (1985) by Neil Postman.

[x] Walter Benjamin (1892 – 1940), German Jewish philosopher and essayist.

[xi] Further reading – *Technics and Civilization* (1934) by Lewis Mumford.

[xii] John Adams (1735 – 1826), American statesman, writer, Founding Father and second president of the United States.

xiii William James (1842 – 1910), American philosopher and psychologist.

xiv Lysenkoism, named for Russian botanist Trofim Denisovich Lysenko (Трофи́м Дени́сович Лысе́нко), was a political doctrine in Joseph Stalin's Soviet Union that mandated that all biological research conducted in the USSR conform to a modified Lamarckian evolutionary theory. The underlying appeal was that it promised a distinct idea of biology based on a view of life that was consistent with the view of human nature insisted upon by Marxist-Leninist dogma. Lysenko was, nonetheless, a thorough fraud - attacking the legitimacy of science for political reasons.

xv Further reading – *Tragic Sense of Life* (1912) by Miguel de Unamuno.

xvi Czesław Miłosz (1911 – 2004), Polish-American poet and diplomat, in 1960 was offered a position as a lecturer at the University of California at Berkeley. He had described how the newness of California perhaps contributed to his feeling of being lost or more uneasy when compared to being back in Poland or Lithuania.

xvii Ludwig Wittgenstein (1889 – 1951), Austrian philosopher. Referenced here in particular for his rejection of metaphysics. It could be said, while I am admiring or sympathetic to Wittgenstein, that his philosophical project was fundamentally a proverbial 'wild goose chase'.

xviii From the poem *Child of Europe* (1946) by Czesław Miłosz.

xix Raymond Aron (1905 – 1983), French philosopher and sociologist.
Albert Camus (1913 – 1960), French author and journalist.
René Char (1907 – 1988), French poet and member of the French Resistance.
Jean Grenier (1898 – 1971), French philosopher and writer.
Arthur Koestler (1905 – 1983), Hungarian British author and journalist.
Czesław Miłosz (1911 – 2004), Polish-American poet and diplomat.
George Orwell (1903 – 1950), English novelist and essayist.
Boris Pasternak (1890 – 1960), Russian poet, novelist, and literary translator.
Ignazio Silone (1900 – 1978), Italian novelist and political leader.
Manès Sperber (1905 – 1984), Austrian-French novelist, essayist and psychologist.
Simone Weil (1909 – 1943), French philosopher, mystic, and political activist.

xx Jacques Ellul (1912 – 1994), French philosopher and author of *Propaganda: The Formation of Men's Attitudes* (1965/1973)

xxi Further reading of Tony Judt.
Postwar: A History of Europe Since 1945. (2005).
Ill Fares the Land (2010).
The Burden of Responsibility: Blum, Camus, Aron, and the French Twentieth Century (1998).
The Memory Chalet (2010)

Thinking the Twentieth Century (2012).
When the Facts Change: Essays, 1995 – 2010. (2015).

[xxii] Aleksandr Solzhenitsyn (1918 – 2008), Russian novelist and historian. Leszek Kołakowski (1927 – 2009), Polish philosopher and historian of ideas.

[xxiii] *The Denial of Death* (1973) by Ernest Becker.

[xxiv] Quote from Theodore Roosevelt. "Get action. Do things; be sane; don't fritter away your time; create, act, take a place wherever you are and be somebody."

[xxv] Quoting myself.

[xxvi] *Pensées* (1670) by Blaise Pascal

Printed in Great Britain
by Amazon